CRITICAL PERSPECTIVES ON LEADERSHIP

Within contemporary culture, 'leadership' is seen in ways that appeal to celebrated societal values and norms. As a result, it is becoming difficult to use the language of leadership without at the same time assuming its essentially positive, intrinsically affirmative nature. Within organizations, routinely referring to bosses as 'leaders' has, therefore, become both a symptom and a cause of a deep, largely unexamined new conceptual architecture. This architecture underpins how we think about authority and power at work. Capitalism, and its turbo-charged offspring neo-liberalism, have effectively captured 'leader' and 'leadership' to serve their own purposes. In other words, organizational leadership today is so often a particular kind of insidious conservativism dressed up in radical adjectives.

This book makes visible the work that the language of leadership does in perpetuating fictions that are useful for bosses of work organizations. We do this so that we – and anyone who shares similar discomforts – can make a start in unravelling the fiction. We contend that even if our views are contrary to the vast and powerful leadership industry, our basic arguments rest on things that are plain and evident for all to see.

Critical Perspectives on Leadership: The Language of Corporate Power will be key reading for students, academics and practitioners in the disciplines of Leadership, Organizational Studies, Critical Management Studies, Sociology and the related disciplines.

Mark Learmonth is Professor of Organization Studies at Durham University, UK. He researches the personal consequences of work.

Kevin Morrell is an Associate Dean at Durham University, UK. He researches how organizations and individuals contribute to the public good.

ROUTLEDGE STUDIES IN LEADERSHIP RESEARCH

6. Revitalising Leadership
Putting Theory and Practice into Context
Suze Wilson, Stephen Cummings, Brad Jackson, and Sarah, Proctor-Thomson

7. Women, Religion and Leadership
Female Saints as Unexpected Leaders
Edited by Barbara Denison

8. "Leadership Matters?"
Finding Voice, Connection and Meaning in the 21st Century
Edited by Chris Mabey and David Knights

9. Innovation in Environmental Leadership
Critical Perspectives
Edited by Benjamin W. Redekop, Deborah Rigling Gallagher, and Rian Satterwhite

10. After Leadership
Edited by Brigid Carroll, Suze Wilson, and Josh Firth

11. Creative Leadership
Contexts and Propsects
Edited by Charalampos Mainemelis, Olga Epitropaki, and Ronit Kark

12. Theoretical Perspectives of Strategic Followership
David Zoogah

13. Good Dividends
Responsible leadership of Business Purpose
Edited by Steve Kempster and Thomas Maak

14. Leading in the Age of Innovations
Change of Values and Approaches
Lenka Theodoulides, Gabriela Kormancová, and David Cole

15. Critical Perspectives on Leadership
The Language of Corporate Power
Mark Learmonth and Kevin Morrell

CRITICAL PERSPECTIVES ON LEADERSHIP

The Language of Corporate Power

Mark Learmonth and Kevin Morrell

Routledge
Taylor & Francis Group
NEW YORK AND LONDON

First published 2019
by Routledge
52 Vanderbilt Avenue, New York, NY 10017

and by Routledge
2 Park Square, Milton Park, Abingdon, Oxon OX14 4RN

Routledge is an imprint of the Taylor & Francis Group, an informa business

© 2019 Taylor & Francis

The right of Mark Learmonth and Kevin Morrell to be identified as authors of this work has been asserted by them in accordance with sections 77 and 78 of the Copyright, Designs and Patents Act 1988.

All rights reserved. No part of this book may be reprinted or reproduced or utilised in any form or by any electronic, mechanical, or other means, now known or hereafter invented, including photocopying and recording, or in any information storage or retrieval system, without permission in writing from the publishers.

Trademark notice: Product or corporate names may be trademarks or registered trademarks, and are used only for identification and explanation without intent to infringe.

Library of Congress Cataloging-in-Publication Data
Names: Learmonth, Mark, author. | Morrell, Kevin, author.
Title: Critical perspectives on leadership : the language of corporate power / Mark Learmonth and Kevin Morrell.
Description: New York, NY : Routledge, 2019. |
Series: Routledge studies in leadership research | Includes bibliographical references and index.
Identifiers: LCCN 2019001027| ISBN 9781138093980 (hardback) | ISBN 9781138093997 (pbk.) | ISBN 9781315105994 (ebook)
Subjects: LCSH: Leadership. | Communication in management.
Classification: LCC HD57.7 .L43765 2019 | DDC 658.4/092014--dc23
LC record available at https://lccn.loc.gov/2019001027

ISBN: 978-1-138-09398-0 (hbk)
ISBN: 978-1-138-09399-7 (pbk)
ISBN: 978-1-315-10599-4 (ebk)

Typeset in Bembo
by Taylor & Francis Books

Printed and bound in Great Britain by
TJ International Ltd, Padstow, Cornwall

CONTENTS

List of Illustrations	*vii*
Acknowledgments	*ix*
Preface	*x*
1 Introducing the Language of Leadership	1

PART I
Against 'Leadership'   **11**

2 Using the Language of Leadership	13
3 Measuring the Language of Leadership	28
4 Polishing Our Chains	33
5 Building Santa's Workshop	43

PART II
'Leadership' as Rhetoric   **55**

6 Labels Matter	57
7 Performing Leadership	70

PART III
The Seductions of 'Leadership' — 81

8 The Attractions of Being (Called) a 'Leader' — 83
9 A Boost to the Executive Ego — 101

PART IV
Resistance — 117

10 What is to be Done? — 119
11 Concluding Thoughts: Leadership as a Fig Leaf? — 135
12 Further Reading — 140

References — *151*
Index — *159*

ILLUSTRATIONS

Figure

11.1	Better World Through Better Leadership	138

Tables

1.1	The Language of Leadership	3
2.1	Leadership Failures	14
2.2	Strong Leadership	14
2.3	Leather-Patched Leaders?	17
3.1	Word Sketch of the Use of 'Leader' in the Early 1990s and 2015: Commonest Modifier of 'Leader'	30
3.2	Word Sketch of the Use of 'Manager' in the Early 1990s and 2015: Commonest Modifier of 'Manager'	31
4.1	From Shop-Floor Worker to Follower; From 'The Management' to Leaders	34
6.1	A Simple Hierarchy of the Sciences	59
6.2	The Linguistic Turn and its Descendants	68
8.1	People Who Some Have Called 'Leaders': Listed in No Particular Order	99
9.1	Me-dership Careers	107
9.2	Word Sketch of the Use of 'Follower' in the Early 1990s and 2015: Commonest Modifier of 'Follower'	111

9.3 Word Sketch of the Use of 'Worker' in the Early 1990s and 2015: Verbs With 'Worker' or 'Follower' as Object   115

12.1 Academic Institutions with the Name 'Management' and Their Subject Areas   145

ACKNOWLEDGMENTS

We are grateful to many people who have contributed to our thinking about (and against) leadership over the years. We should start by thanking David Varley at Routledge who invited us to write this book while he was Commissioning Editor for Business, Management and Accounting research. We would also like to mention the people who very generously undertook to read an early version of the full draft and who provided us with insightful comments: Todd Bridgman, David Clough, John Edmonds, Jon Harding, Mike Humphreys, Mike Klein, James Preece and Suze Wilson. In addition, Jackie Ford, Nancy Harding, Hugh Lee and Philip Warwick deserve special thanks for their ongoing comments and ideas in many informal conversations. We would also like to thank Gerlinde Mautner for introducing us to corpus linguistics. Naturally, all the views (and errors) in the book remain our own.

Finally, we are enormously grateful to our immediate families for their support during the writing of this book. Mark thanks Glynis, James and Katie. Kevin thanks Sarah, Emily, Ruby and Jake.

PREFACE

Who Is This Book For

If you have ever been suspicious or cynical about the use of terms like 'leader' and 'leadership', we have written this book for you. You are in good company if you are suspicious of leadership. Here is one of the things that the novelist George Orwell wrote about the leadership of Napoleon the pig in his famous novel, *Animal Farm*:

> It had become usual to give Napoleon the credit for every successful achievement and every stroke of good fortune. You would often hear one hen remark to another, 'Under the guidance of our Leader, Comrade Napoleon, I have laid five eggs in six days'; or two cows, enjoying a drink at the pool, would exclaim, 'Thanks to the leadership of Comrade Napoleon, how excellent this water tastes!' (Orwell, 1945/2000: 67–8)

You may have sat through a leadership development course, doubting any magical transformation into 'leader' would happen to you or those around you; doubting any magical transformation, even though most of the other people on the course, like the animals in *Animal Farm*, seem to be buying in to it all. Perhaps you have had to re-describe your job and work experiences using a 'leadership competency' framework. Maybe you are tired of the latest banalities from the treadmill of 'leadership research'. Or perhaps you are cynical, in the same sort of way that Orwell appears to have been, because when you think about the people running your organization it seems bizarre they could be described as 'leaders'. It could even be that in your own work you have been called a 'leader', or you have been told to 'show leadership' – and rather than thinking 'at last!' – felt uncomfortable. Or perhaps you heard a colleague being described as a leader and thought to yourself 'who – *them*?' If you think that when people talk about leadership at work it is over-the-top or even silly, this book will definitely interest you. It shows how this language is not simply over-the-top and absurd, but also dangerous.

Our book sets out a detailed, forensic account of what is happening when people use this language at work – what we call the 'language of leadership'. We wrote this book because we are interested in the way relationships between people can be changed simply by calling someone 'leader'. We also think calling someone 'leader' brings about changes in how people think of themselves. By saying that we are critical of 'leadership' and using scare quotes round the term leadership, we mean that we are being critical of the language of leadership as it is generally used, particularly as it is used at work. However, it is worth pointing out that the use of 'leader' and 'leadership' has seeped through and affected almost every area of modern life.

One thing we do is poke fun at the very idea of leadership itself. In a secular, consumerist society, leadership seems to be one of the few things to remain holy. People may regularly question 'leaders', but very few ever question the need for 'leadership'. Our attack on this modern sacred cow is worthwhile if only because it is something a lot of other writers and academics take very seriously. To us, there is something irresistibly comic about the moral earnestness in so much of the writing that calls for 'better leadership' in organizational life.

One absurd implication of the spread of this language is that in all walks of life we are now surrounded by people doing ordinary jobs who are called leaders. They are expected to demonstrate leadership somehow as an explicit requirement of their role. Rather than being a title as it was used traditionally (generally reserved for figures who changed history) nowadays on your morning run to get milk you could pass dozens of 'leaders' – on their way to jobs in manufacturing, retail, marketing or any other sector. While you are in the supermarket's dairy aisle, you may see the 'team leader' of that section. For instance, one of the UK's major supermarkets recently advertised jobs using an instore poster that read:

> **LEADING STARTS HERE**. We're now hiring Customer and Trading managers. Starting salary of at least £25,000. We'll help you to be the leader you want to be, speak to a member of the instore team today (Sainsbury's, 2018; emphasis in original).

This rash of 'leaders' and of 'leadership' roles does not ever really get called into question, even though twenty or thirty years ago the same kinds of people were in the same kinds of roles, doing the same kinds of jobs and were called (mere) managers. 'Manager' is a term that is still also used, as you can see in the above advert – but in a much lower profile and more mundane way than 'leader'. If you think it is strange to suggest we have more leaders in society nowadays and you want to know why, this book will interest you because this is one of the questions we answer when dissecting the language of leadership.

Speaking to people in different organizations, we know we are not alone in being cynical about 'leadership' in this way. Other writers are outspoken critics of claims for the value of leaders and the need for leadership in organizations – take for example the book *Decoding Leadership Bullshit* (O'Ween, 2013). However, such cynicism often has to be hidden – there is a need to be 'on-message' in many organizations. Cynicism about 'leadership' might not ever be voiced because it signals implied criticism of top bosses. Indeed, it is hard to be definitive about how many feel this way because it is generally wiser to voice anti-leadership opinions behind closed doors.

To be critical of 'leadership' in the sort of radical way we argue for in this book – to be 'against leadership' as we put it in the first part of the book – is also to attack some sacred truths about corporate life. For instance, as the quote from *Animal Farm* illustrates, it is typically assumed that when an organization experiences success it is the result of 'leadership'. Success is never, in other words, just down to good luck, or a result of other people's failures, or a consequence of having superior resources, or a product of work intensification, or the ability to capitalize on inequalities. A similar sacred cow is that the most senior person in a corporation or public sector organization is a 'leader' rather than merely a more senior colleague.

Being 'against leadership' in this way is perhaps particularly likely to make us unpopular with some gurus and academics who have made their living from the 'leadership industry'. In fact it has already made us unpopular even with some who would describe themselves as critics of this industry. In the last few years, both of us have taken a much more oppositional stance in relation to the language of leadership. Writing this book, which is definitively *against* 'leadership', is the culmination of thinking that has crystallized from a somewhat less hard-line, if always relatively critical position on leadership. That said, there has always been something about the cultural associations of terms like 'leader' and 'follower' that we have tried to resist, especially in the context of work organizations and when thinking about our own work experiences. These terms sound a bit daft to us. Unfortunately, even if the terms are absurd, they are also toxic.

Throughout our own careers we have never thought of ourselves as 'leaders'. Neither have we ever aspired to 'leadership'. Just as we think many other people will, we both tend to resist suggestions that we are – using current, everyday jargon – occupying 'leadership roles'. Even where the waffle of leadership is expected as par for the course we tend to struggle because – basically – we don't like the word 'leader' or what it implies. One of us had a car crash of a (not especially senior) academic job interview when the opening question by the bright-eyed, bushy-tailed chair of the panel was, 'can you tell me about your leadership style?' Even though he was expecting the de rigueur verbiage that we all get in job interviews, the fact the panel chair took such an empty-headed question seriously and indeed 'led' with it as their starter for ten seemed absurd.

Our Aims

We are not simply motivated by wanting to be awkward. There are decent intellectual reasons to be cynical about 'leadership'. When used at work, the language of leadership has at its heart a misleading and dangerous lie. This is the fiction that – because 'leaders' and 'followers' are, by definition, on the same side – companies can maximize profits (and public sector bodies can make big savings) whilst benefiting *everyone* involved; even their lowest paid workers. Unfortunately, this particular circle can rarely, if ever, be squared. Leadership in corporate life has become an ingratiating mask, disguising an unseemly scramble for power and wealth. It enables corporate bosses and other elites to portray and imagine themselves as inherently virtuous. In fact, we think one measure of the profound change in Western society over the last thirty years or so – the shift towards what is often called neo-liberalism – is that the language of leadership has spread so widely and become taken for granted. It is becoming a language that is now nearly inescapable for talking (or even thinking) about power in organizational life.

As we have said, an important part of what we try to do is to poke fun at this language and labels like 'leader'. At the same time as doing this, we also want to show why we think this language can be dangerous. We are not interested in ridiculing any one person, and indeed we often go to some lengths to anonymize people whom we quote directly, but what we want to ridicule is a series of what seem to us absurd ideas and associations. These come bundled with this leadership language and often make very little sense.

We have little doubt that some people who use the language of leadership have honourable personal and political motives for doing so. Nevertheless, as George Orwell once commented in his book *Politics and the English Language*, '[t]he invasion of one's mind by readymade phrases ... can only be prevented if one is constantly on guard against them' (1945/2013: 16). There are risks if 'leadership' and 'leader' are entirely normalized. They now seem to be the readymade way to speak about those with power in organizational life. This means that we risk complicity in the flattery and glamorization of organizational elites, at the expense of the rest of us. Orwell's *Animal Farm* is, in part, a dramatic account of the degenerate effects of the language of leadership as it gradually invades the animals' minds. This happens in the mind of Napoleon (the chief pig who came to be called the leader), just as much as in the minds of the rest of the animals.

We are also indebted to Orwell more fundamentally for his insights into how political, economic and social power depends on the manipulation of language. This is particularly evident in *1984*, his most famous novel. The book's chilling account of 'doublethink' and 'newspeak' shows how language can be twisted to disguise or even invert phenomena to make them appear more palatable (e.g. 'war is peace', 'freedom is slavery', 'ignorance is strength'). The ultimate aim of newspeak is to make any kind of heresy unthinkable. Seen in this light, our book is intended as a kind of heresy against the language of leadership. Our subtitle, 'The Language of

Corporate Power' is a reminder of Orwell's insights into language – and a caution against how these can be subverted in the interests of those in power.

One of our aims is exactly as Orwell encourages: to be on our guard against 'leadership', especially in work settings. The language of leadership has an insidious capacity to invade our minds and our imaginations in ways we hardly notice. This language is often used unthinkingly and yet whenever we do this it is at our peril. The language of leadership strongly supports corporate power, feeding our culture of neo-liberalism. This is a culture that celebrates competition and markets and in doing so it relies on useful fictions. These include the idea that anyone can succeed if they compete strongly enough. It is a useful fiction because the cards are stacked against the poor and the weak, but a belief in fair meritocracy simply perpetuates systems that consistently reward elites.

A related aim is that we hope our dissection of the language of leadership will help others to stay sane and distanced when working in an environment where this language has taken hold. Our book is designed to inspire people, especially those working in 'leadership'-saturated environments, to think more critically about labels like 'leader'. This is an important aim because these readymade labels now seem unavoidable in organizational life – and indeed they are contaminating almost all spheres of human activity.

We also want to emphasize that we would like you to enjoy our dissection of the language of leadership and to enjoy sharing in our version of active, purposeful cynicism. We hope the book may help you have a greater appreciation for your own cynical instincts and to realize that any suspicion or unease you may have about uses of 'leadership' is well placed. You will find plenty of support and validation for such doubts here.

1

INTRODUCING THE LANGUAGE OF LEADERSHIP

This book takes a stand against the rise of what we call the 'language of leadership' in organizational life. We use the phrase 'language of leadership' to signal the way in which some people (bosses or others with authority in organizational life) are now *routinely* referred to as 'leaders'; just as what they do routinely gets called 'leadership'.

At first glance, whether we call bosses 'leaders' – or anything else – might seem a relatively trivial matter. But because they are used so routinely, the terms 'leader' and 'leadership' are becoming foundational in our thinking. Indeed, these terms perhaps feature in our everyday talk about work organizations – before we do any thinking. Here it is worth recalling Orwell's caution we referred to in the Preface to be on our guard against readymade phrases. The language of leadership is made up of readymade phrases that have invaded everyday talk and they pre-package the world of work. They frame some fundamental, taken-for-granted beliefs about power and organizational life.

Within contemporary culture, 'leadership' is seen in ways that appeal to celebrated societal values and norms. As a result, it is becoming difficult to use any of this language of leadership without at the same time assuming its essentially positive, intrinsically affirmative nature. Routinely referring to bosses as 'leaders' has, therefore, become both a symptom and a cause of a deep, largely unexamined new conceptual architecture. This architecture underpins how we think about authority and power at work. Capitalism, and its turbo-charged offspring neo-liberalism, seem to have effectively captured 'leader' and 'leadership'. Capitalism and neo-liberalism are both associated with competition and individualism and both make inequality at work natural or even a cause for celebration. The account of authority and power provided by the language of leadership boosts the status of the elite bosses, while at the same time it has been important in legitimating pay cuts and the precarious conditions of work for those near the bottom of the pile.

These are all reasons that we are critical of 'leadership' – because we see the language of leadership as something that has been hijacked by managerial elites. We are not necessarily critical of the phenomenon of leadership itself – in the sense in which the term has more traditionally been used however. Along with some major social theorists who have written about leadership (e.g. Max Weber and Sigmund Freud) we have no problem with calling someone a leader if they genuinely have 'followers' and can therefore legitimately claim to be among the ranks of people such as eminent politicians, religious or military figures and the like. 'Having followers' is, for us, one of the basic criteria someone needs to meet for 'leader' to be a meaningful and appropriate term. The trouble is that bosses of work organizations are very rarely leaders in this conventional sense. As far as most workplaces are concerned, as survey after survey has consistently shown, more people hate their bosses than admire them. According to a recent Gallup poll for instance, 'eighty-five percent of workers worldwide admit to hating their jobs when surveyed anonymously ... many people in the world hate their job and especially their boss' (Return to Now, 2017). Even fewer workers would consider that they 'follow' their bosses. Indeed, it is for this reason that in Chapter 9 we argue that calling workers 'followers' is most likely to be considered an insult to workers themselves.

The Language of Leadership

Our use of the phrase, 'language of leadership' is different from some other uses. More typically, when people say the 'language of leadership' they mean something like tips on how to persuade (or manipulate) people. It can mean how to sound like a leader; or what to say in front of a mirror that will make you believe that you are a leader; or even how to stand – what 'power pose' to adopt perhaps. When we use the 'language of leadership', we are referring to a sub-vocabulary that is invading corporate life (and life elsewhere). Some examples of terms from the language of leadership in the sense we mean are shown in Table 1.1.

We are not simply using the phrase 'language of leadership' to pick out the specific cluster of terms in Table 1.1. In any case, the table is not an exhaustive list of phrases. Nor are any of these phrases necessarily wrong in any way. Any one of them could be being used appropriately by authors or people describing a setting. Despite our cynicism about the language of leadership we are also not suggesting that when any of these terms are used that our eyes should simply glaze over and that we ought to disregard whatever is said next because it is bound to be nonsense (though it often is close to being nonsense in our experience).

Even though we have set the table out in this way, the 'language of leadership' does not just mean a bundle of terms that can be used to refer to a quality or a role, or practice, or person or process, or to describe a set of characteristics or behaviours in any given situation. Instead, we are critical of the language of leadership for a broader reason. The cynicism we have about these readymade terms is motivated by a simple, but powerful idea: that these words 'do' things. In saying that terms do things we

TABLE 1.1 The Language of Leadership

Core terms	Leader, Lead, Leading, Leadership (and even 'Leaderful') referring to a role, person, activity, quality or process
The kind of person or process or style of being a leader or kind of leadership	Adaptive Leader, Altruistic Leader, Autocratic Leader, Authentic Leader, Benevolent Leader, Change Leader, Character Leader, Charismatic Leader, Coaching Leader, Collaborative Leader, Cross-cultural Leader, CSR Leader, Democratic Leader, Differentiated Leader, Distributed Leader, Embodied Leader, Empowering Leader, Ethical Leader, Integrative Leader, Laissez-faire Leader, Participative Leader, People-oriented Leader, Positive Leader, Primal Leader, Purpose-driven Leader, Relational Leader, Safety Leader, Self-Leader, Servant Leader, Social Justice Leader, Spiritual Leader, Strategic Leader, Strong Leader, Task-oriented Leader, Team Leader, Thought Leader, Transactional Leader, Transformational Leader, Transformative Leader (in this list, wherever it says leader we can also have leadership)
Jobs that are a	Leadership ... Challenge / Opportunity / Position / Role / Task / Vacancy
A training activity	Leadership ... Awareness / Building / Coaching / Development / Mentoring / Mindfulness / Training
A 'real' quality	Authentic ... / Have a Track Record of ... / Have Proven ... / Showed ... / Genuine ... / Real ... / True ... 'Leadership' (which concedes that a lot of what could be called 'leadership' is not real in any conventional way of thinking about the real.)
Jobs require you to	Demonstrate ... / Display ... / Embody ... / Role Model ... / Show ... Leadership
A kind of follower or followership	Activist / Bystander / Alienated / Collaborator / Colluder / Conformer / Courageous / Diehard / Dynamic / Isolate / Leader-centric / Loyal / Pragmatic / Star / Sheep / Yes-person ... Follower(ship)
Terms that imply a leader or the need for leadership	Vison / Values / Hearts and Minds / Strategy / True North / Compass-setting / Direction-setting / Path-breaking and – most basically perhaps – Change

mean they are not purely descriptive. Instead, the very act of calling something 'leadership', or calling someone a 'leader', or using any of the terms in Table 1.1 or similar terms – actually changes the nature of that situation. As we explain in more detail in Chapters 6 and 7, the words that we use to describe the social world also create our world. Each of the terms and phrases from the language of leadership in Table 1.1 'does' things when it is used to describe the world of work.

This distinction between describing the social world and creating the social world is what motivates Orwell's caution that we be on our guard against readymade phrases. It is crucial when it comes to dissecting terms like 'leader' and 'leadership' because it is through ordinary, day-to-day language that we create the world at work. These terms come bundled with assumptions about how we should understand relations of power in work organizations. Throughout the book, we identify and challenge these assumptions. We unravel the language of leadership by identifying the connotations and associations 'leader' and 'leadership' have in contemporary organizational life. We explore these and explain how they affect those who become called 'leaders' and those who they might believe they lead.

There are contradictions and tensions that come bundled with terms like 'leader' and 'leadership'. On the one hand, these terms are used in ways that suggest people called 'leaders' are in positions of unquestioned power and authority. On the other hand, the overwhelmingly positive associations to the terms 'leader' and 'leadership' suggest organizational leaders are 'good' or 'nice' in some way. Unlike 'managers' – whom we might even expect to have occasional conflict with their subordinates – 'leaders' must have followers for the term 'leader' to make sense. 'Leaders' at work are, by definition, on the same side as those they lead – or else why would they deserve the title? As Jeffrey Pfeffer (2015a) has pointed out:

> Over the last several decades, the [leadership] industry has produced a recipe for how to be a successful corporate leader: Be trustworthy and authentic, serve others (particularly those who work for and with you), be modest, and exhibit empathetic understanding and emotional intelligence.

The routine, readymade uses of 'leader' and 'leadership' are redrawing our picture of relations at work. What these terms 'do' goes beyond describing people who are in positions of power and authority. Instead, the use of these terms creates and justifies a particular kind of relationship. This has two aspects: flattering bosses and flattening workers – the core themes of this book.

Flattering Bosses

The first aspect to the readymade uses of these terms is that talking about bosses as leaders overly flatters them and excessively glamourizes their roles. As mentioned, this is because the title 'leader' has connotations of an authority and power that goes unquestioned. To call someone 'leader' implies more than that they have been appointed to a formal position of authority. It suggests there is something 'special' about them and their authority. This implication airbrushes away the kind of conflict at work that we might associate with the term manager. For this reason, one of the important consequences of the rise in the language of leadership is that the people who used to think of themselves as mere 'managers' can now imagine themselves using a term that makes them sound much grander and considerably more important. They can imagine themselves as 'leaders'.

The following quote by John Hendry (2013: 96–7) captures the ways in which many people imagine what it must be like to be a 'manager':

> For most managers, management is basically a job ... Few people become managers ... out of a sense of vocation. It is not something they do out of a burning desire to express themselves, to contribute to society or humanity, or to take a stand on issues that matter to them. A successful manager ... might well be proud of her achievements, but being a manager ... is rarely in itself a source of great pride. ... It is a job, and a good and respectable job, and for many people an interesting and/or remunerative one, but at the end of the day it's just a job.

In contrast, Gianpiero and Jennifer Petriglieri (Petriglieri and Petriglieri, 2015: 631) show us how today's dominant cultural image of the organizational leader is rather different:

> The image of leadership that predominates is of an individual ascending to, or occupying, a position of hierarchical power, competently adapting to his or her environment, and wielding his or her influence to achieve financial (or otherwise measurable) results and, in so doing, rising further up the ladder. ... [thus, this image] portray[s] leaders as 'crafters of their own fortunes' ... in a world where success – usually defined as promotions and profits – hinges on making the right decisions in high-stake situations ... a worldview in which individualism and heroism prevail.

When we call one person a leader and another person a manager, we are not just naming them differently. While managers are generally imagined as bureaucrats, leaders are imagined to be admired by their followers, shareholders and market analysts alike; imagined too, as being able to transform organizations and those who work for them as they pursue their visionary strategies (Wilson, 2016). In other words, a key reason the language of leadership has become popular is because it has suited the interests of those who represent corporate power – the bosses. This language has become a pro-elite resource; a kind of filter through which elites can imagine and project their identities in much more positive (and functionally useful) ways than was the case with the language of management.

Flattening Workers

The second way in which the language of leadership is redrawing social relations is perhaps even more important. 'Leaders' at work, by definition, have the same goals as their so-called 'followers'; although 'leaders' set these goals. Yet the language of leadership is often a mask or disguise because – plainly – those in positions of power often have different and incompatible interests to those lower down the organizational hierarchy. Routinely using 'leader' is almost a form of permission that allows this disguise to persist. It can make us turn our eyes away from wider injustices that many so-called leaders benefit from.

Over the last thirty years or so, one of the huge ironies of the growth in popularity of the term 'leader', as we examine in more detail in Chapter 4, is that it has occurred at the same time as there has been a massive deterioration in pay, job security and working conditions for many ordinary workers. This widening gap undercuts any idea that there are more harmonious relations between 'leaders' and their supposed 'followers'. On the contrary, the deterioration in ordinary workers' pay has directly benefited senior staff in terms of pay rises at the top. Often such pay rises are also conditional on 'efficiency gains' or what we might call work intensification.

When we redraw this picture and redescribe managers as leaders, we are reshaping the ways in which we imagine organizational elites. The overwhelmingly positive cultural images and associations surrounding the term 'leadership' are reshaping the image of bosses. This is done in a way that is not simply glamourizing and flattering to them, but that also actively serves their wider political and financial interests, in the process denying the interests of ordinary workers.

'Leadership' is Terminally Toxic

Given the pro-elite associations of 'leader' and 'leadership', we see the language of leadership at work as terminally toxic. Rather than try to reinvent or detoxify it – something that has been proposed most recently by Carroll, Firth and Wilson (2019) – we argue that we should simply stop using the term 'leader' when referring to bosses. The language of leadership is irredeemably flawed; but it is also unnecessary – plenty of alternatives are available. Anyone interested in progressive ideas about organizational life should simply stop using the term. Otherwise, *whenever* we use the term 'leader' in the workplace, and regardless of our intention in doing so, it is casting a vote of support for bosses. In the process, we are also casting a vote *against* the traditional interests of workers.

Sadly though, the language of leadership is increasingly popular: in the corporate world, in the media, in daily workplace conversations and even in everyday, non-work life. Most worryingly of all to us, if only because it is perhaps the place where it can be challenged most readily, it is on the rise in academia – with researchers who study work organizations. This includes, in a strange paradox, much research that claims to be critical of leadership. More widely, people seem ever happier to make sense of the nature of work, and much of our wider lives, using this readymade, toxic language. In the process, we are providing a kind of support to the inequalities which uses of 'leader' and 'leadership' cover up. Though the use of this language is often absurd, it is also dangerous – and this is what this book seeks to challenge.

Structure of the Book

Part I: Against 'Leadership'

The first part of the book shows how the use of the language of leadership has dramatically increased in recent years. We also examine its troubling effects in more detail.

In Chapter 2, 'Using the Language of Leadership' we start to chart the rise and rise of the language of leadership. Today, it is not just corporations, but football teams, schools and families who are said to have 'leaders'. Often the term 'leader' is reserved for high-status individuals, but what seems particularly strange to us is that even junior academics on temporary contracts increasingly have to 'show leadership' (whatever that might mean); at least they do according to their job descriptions.

In Chapter 3, 'Measuring the Language of Leadership', we show how there has been a marked shift in the way we talk about leaders. We do this by analysing the British National Corpus and the English Web 2015 (enTenTen15) – two collections of huge numbers of samples of written and spoken language from a wide range of sources. These are chosen to represent a wide cross-section of British English. Our analysis shows that whereas in the early 1990s the term 'leader' was used mainly for politicians, by 2015, this political use of the term had been overtaken by its use in business.

In Chapter 4, 'Polishing our Chains', we take some specific examples of how the term 'leader' is used to show why the rise and rise in the language of leadership matters. One of the things we suggest is that the title leader (while it is clearly not the whole story) may well have contributed to bosses getting away with huge pay rises – while ordinary workers have had their pay cut and their working conditions made more precarious. We argue this is because the language of leadership seems to be changing the wider cultural climate – making it much friendlier towards the interests of elites. At the same time, the language of leadership is also making the climate increasingly hostile for people who find themselves doing part-time and precarious work: this is the dynamic of flattering the bosses and flattening the workers.

In Chapter 5, 'Building Santa's Workshop', we examine the basic nature of the employment relationship and argue that there is conflict at the heart of this relationship. This conflict arises because bosses (as representative of owners) and workers often have fundamentally opposing aims. Maximising profits almost inevitably means extracting extra value from workers – and at least for some increased insecurity and worsened conditions. The traditional terms 'manager' and 'worker' tacitly acknowledge such conflict and a divergence of interests. In contrast, the language of leadership seeks to make the workplace into a kind of 'Santa's workshop', where everyone below the leader is imagined (against common-sense) to be a happy elf. We also develop some of the ideas in the opening chapters to speculate on why 'leadership' has become the routine way in which we talk about the exercise of power, authority and influence in organizations. We show how this state of affairs is not just absurd or ridiculous, but also dangerous. It is dangerous because, most basically, the language of leadership glosses over sources of contest and resistance.

Part II: Leadership as Rhetoric

The second part of the book anchors our claims in some of the most exciting ideas that inform our understanding of language.

In Chapter 6, 'Labels Matter', we flesh out one of the central ideas in the book – that the language of leadership is not just describing the world of work but is actually building and creating this world. We introduce concepts from the social sciences (disciplines such as sociology and social psychology) and the humanities (disciplines like literary studies and history) – for instance the roles of rhetoric, self-fulfilling prophecies and narrative. These concepts all help to explain the processes through which the language of leadership has such toxic effects. Bringing in concepts from the humanities is especially helpful because for so many academics who study leadership, their overwhelming preoccupation is with 'science'. This bias has resulted in blind spots when it comes to understanding leadership that this book, in part, is intending to remedy.

In Chapter 7, 'Performing Leadership', we continue with these explorations into the nature and effects of language use. Having considered a number of disciplinary perspectives in Chapter 6, we look in more detail at how insights from philosophy can be applied to understand the effects of the language of leadership. To do this we draw on the work of John Austin and Michel Foucault among others. In different ways, both these thinkers have informed our understanding of how language is never purely descriptive but has direct effects on the social world.

Part III: The Seductions of Leadership

In this section, we bring together ideas from the first two parts of the book to show why the language of leadership has taken hold of so much of organizational life.

In Chapter 8, 'The Attractions of Being (Called) a "Leader"', we look in more detail at some of the images that the readymade language of leadership calls to mind. We argue that simply talking about 'leadership' at work means we almost inevitably talk in positive terms. To explain this we look at three of the major sources from which images of organizational leaders are drawn: (i) the military officer, (ii) political and world leaders, and perhaps a little more surprisingly (iii) 'hippie' leaders.

Chapter 9, 'A Boost to the Executive Ego', sets out how the positive associations surrounding leadership benefit elites. Although some ideas associated with leadership (such as creating a common vision) could theoretically help workers at all levels of the organization, this language has been largely co-opted and put to work in promoting the interests of those in power. One curious symptom of this is found in the aspirational, self-serving language people use on social media when positioning themselves as leaders. We call this 'me-dership' (a term adapted from the LinkedIn satirist Mike Winnet). We also unpick the idea of 'followership', suggesting that this is an ugly, patronising term and far more destructive than the traditional, solidarity-conferring term 'worker'.

Part IV: Resistance

In the final part of the book, we look at what prospects there may be for struggling against the language of leadership.

In Chapter 10, 'What is to be Done?', we speculate about how we might resist the language of leadership. We begin with discussing some attempts to guard against the negative effects of leadership language. We see these as well intended but ultimately likely to fail because they still rely on the language of leadership. These include versions of so-called critical leadership studies, as well as forms of women's leadership and collective leadership. Our preference is to try to avoid the language of leadership altogether. We end the chapter with stories of some of our own attempts at avoiding the language of leadership in our own (leadership-saturated) industry.

In Chapter 11, 'Concluding Thoughts: Leadership as a Fig Leaf?', we sum up our arguments, and look forward to the future. The struggle we advocate is certainly an uphill one because of how institutionalised the language of leadership has become. Also, given that this pro-elite language serves the interest of the powerful it is likely to remain institutionalised. While we are realistic about prospects for success, we are not entirely pessimistic. We think it is possible to be optimistic, at least about the long run prospects for the decline in the use of the language of leadership. Perhaps alongside its growing use, an increasing number of people are coming to see that 'leadership' is really little more than a fig leaf for corporate elites – hiding the more oppressive aspects of life at work.

Finally, in Chapter 12 'Further Reading' we provide a resource for any readers who would like to explore the themes we have examined in this book further. It includes a relatively brief listing of some additional sources that is perhaps more in the style of an appendix than a conventional chapter. We end with some questions for further research that are also critical of 'leadership' in the same sort of way as we have been.

PART I
Against 'Leadership'

2
USING THE LANGUAGE OF LEADERSHIP

To begin our account, Table 2.1 shows a list of headlines used in recent stories in the UK media. All these stories have been labelled 'leadership failures':

Without going into detail on any of these stories, it is interesting to see how 'leadership failure' refers not just to individuals but to organizations, and not just to particular decisions but also to patterns of working as well as prevailing trends. They relate both to one-off events and systemic phenomena; to business practices, corporations, governments, state and civil society actors. We can also find a comparable list of 'successes' that are said to be down to leadership. We can show this with a quick search of news stories and features that include the phrase 'strong leadership' in Table 2.2.

These headlines also indicate that when we are examining 'leadership' we are working with a very broad and unfocused term, at least as it is used in the media. Once more, there is a similarly broad mix of individuals and organizations. We could again draw a distinction between prevailing patterns or a general climate and between one-off events or problems. Both these sets of headlines give us a very small indication of how institutionalized and taken-for-granted the language of leadership now is – in organizational life and beyond. Furthermore, it seems as if 'leadership' (whatever it might turn out to be) is positioned as the answer to everything.

If we wanted to base our sense of what 'leadership' is on these headlines, we would sign up to some very loose and general ideas. Leadership would seem to be something that is in some way 'special' or 'powerful'. Just as generally, leadership can be understood as something that you want to be 'good' or 'strong', and in that way it is responsible for 'success'. Conversely when things go wrong this can seemingly be explained by 'leadership failure'. This seems to fit Orwell's sense of a readymade phrase perfectly. However, although these headlines show these uses of leadership are clearly commonplace, they also show that the language of leadership is only a

TABLE 2.1 Leadership Failures

British Airways and a Failure in Leadership

Tesco saw a Failure in Leadership

A Failure in Leadership, All the Way Up the Ranks (referring to the torture and abuse of prisoners at Abu Ghraib)

Celtic accuse Scottish FA of Failure in Leadership

Pelosi: Trump Gets F for Failure in Leadership

A Failure in Leadership: The Incompetence of India's Prime Minister

ScotRail Franchise: Failure of Leadership from Transport Minister

The Flint Water Crisis: A Failure of Leadership

America's Gun Violence Represents A Failure Of Leadership, Not Laws

Talking Over People's Heads = Leadership Failure (from an article gloriously titled: 'Science Says This Is the Optimal IQ to Be Considered a Good Leader').

TABLE 2.2 Strong Leadership

London needs Strong Leadership to root out Harassment

Vladimir Putin praises Donald Trump's Strong Leadership

Xi Jinping's Strong Leadership Style has its Risks, but also Advantages

CQC [the Care Quality Commission] calls for Improved Leadership in Mental Health Review

Strong Leadership and Wise Heads Required to Finalise Brexit deal

Want to be a Better Leader? Get Inside Your Head

Halting Population Decline 'Doable' with Strong Leadership, Innovative Ideas

Ofsted Inspectors find 'Child-focussed' Practice, 'Aspirational' Leadership and 'Innovations' in Technology

---

short step from vagueness or even nonsense. After all, you would always want people, organizations or systems to be special and good and to succeed.

Eleven Leaders Out There

We can show the borderline incoherence of leadership language by seeing how it is used in everyday life. For example, below is an extract from a recent interview with a UK Premiership football (i.e. soccer) coach. He was expressing his ambitions for signing a new player in an upcoming transfer window and told the BBC that he wanted a defensive player with 'leadership qualities'. As well as identifying the need for a leader in defence he then went on to say this about leadership:

> That's important in a goalkeeper, that's important in a central midfield player and you'd like to think that you'd have eleven leaders out there.

This seems a logical consequence to a very loose and general sense of leadership – as something 'special' and 'good' which leads to 'success'. As a coach and fan, you would always want players to be 'leaders out there' if all this means is generally being good at football. More generally, in any walk of life you would always want people to be special and good in some way. But then it also strikes us as absurd and – if this is not too much of a contradiction in terms – it is because of this absurdity that it is worth taking this readymade language seriously.

In a team of eleven players, all of whom are leaders, who are they actually leading? Are they all leading each other, or are they taking it in turns to lead, or are they leading at different things? Or are they leading the fans perhaps, who are after all only watching? Anyone who listens to football commentaries will hear this language of leadership sewn throughout the game now. Goalkeepers are often said not just to need to organize their defences when there is a corner, but to need to 'show leadership' – i.e. they need to shout at their team mates to tell them where to stand. Even a clearance header can be described as 'good leadership'. This is not confined to football of course – in a recent episode of the UK talent show *Strictly Come Dancing* one judge criticized a male celebrity dancer for not 'showing leadership'.

Perhaps it seems trivial in sport or entertainment, and football punditry has never been a gold standard for coherence. Unfortunately, the use of this language becomes slightly more meaningful – and therefore more troubling – when we see how it is used in other domains. Online, you can find advice on '10 ways to be your family's leader', on 'becoming a successful and effective parent leader' and on how to take 'parental responsibility for leadership' for example. You can even learn from parents who have been 'great leaders in family life'. One of our friends was recently invited to a training course run by his employer on 'leadership at work and beyond'.

In the same sort of vein, while writing this book, one of us was at a school assembly where 8-year-old children were receiving praise and awards for their achievements during the school year. Daniel (not his real name), was one child who was singled out and praised for 'showing leadership' which clearly made him and his family extremely proud. At this assembly we were told that what Daniel had done was encourage his classmates to make sure they changed into the appropriate footwear for a lesson in PE (physical education). Apparently, one day some children had been so excited they wanted to run outside while wearing their school shoes, but Daniel had reminded them to put their trainers on first. Does it make any sense at all to label what Daniel did 'leadership'?

Perhaps it does in light of the fact that UK schools are evaluated and assessed explicitly on whether they provide an environment that fosters leadership. The schools inspector in the UK, Ofsted, also specifically examines schools' 'leadership teams'. Even the Church of England has leadership development for its clergy (Green, 2014). Similarly, in reviews of medical practice, nurses and doctors do not just keep up to date with their training; they now 'show clinical leadership'.

Even leather-patch-elbowed geeks like us – academics – are no longer simply in the business of trying to publish and teach students. Instead, we are supposed to be 'demonstrating academic leadership'; though we must admit that neither of us really knows what 'demonstrating academic leadership' means we should actually be doing.

Leather-Patch-Elbowed Leaders?

Universities are an interesting place to look at the language of leadership at work. This will also mean we can share some examples from our own work experiences. It will help if we first offer a very quick and rough introduction to academic work in UK Higher Education (HE).

Speaking in broad terms, there are three main areas of work that academics undertake: (i) research, (ii) administration and (iii) teaching. Academic roles tend to involve some combination of these three different areas with, at times, a near exclusive focus on one of them. Again in very broad terms, a hierarchy in terms of the seniority of academic jobs (using UK titles) might go from: (i) lecturer or assistant professor or teaching fellow, (ii) senior lecturer or associate professor or senior/principal teaching fellow, and then (iii) professor. For simplicity, we are missing a lot of roles out and we are not going into any of the nuances about what these mean. Also the terminology and status of these varies from institution to institution.

Almost everywhere now in our occupational context of HE 'leadership' is explicitly mentioned as a desirable, or even necessary characteristic for job applicants. It is also used to describe different activities that are needed to carry out a job. Using the vocabulary of recruitment and selection, these two ways of setting out what is needed to fill a vacancy would respectively be called:

(A) a person specification

and

(B) a role description.

If we combine these two elements together, then for a great many vacancies now (in research, teaching, administration and at any level), it seems that (A) the person filling that vacancy needs to be (in some way) a 'leader' and also that (B) the job they will be doing requires (in some way) 'leadership'. In our experience, this requirement for 'leadership' was not made, even ten years ago.

The most straightforward way to show how the term 'leadership' is used in this context is by looking at some job advertisements. The descriptions in Table 2.3, which are from just one week of adverts for vacancies in teaching and/or research roles in business schools were all featured on the careers website jobs.ac.uk. This is the main source of information on job vacancies in UK HE. It is not important to read these in any depth or detail, and we have in any case not included the name of the institution to preserve some level of confidentiality.

TABLE 2.3 Leather-Patched Leaders?

Title of Job	Extracts from person specification and job description
Lecturer in Transportation Planning and Management	Support subject leaders to make important achievements in academic research Provide leadership in the latest advances in academic research (national and international) Experience as a Research Leader
Senior Lecturer in Logistics and Supply Chain Management	Lead a number of established professionally accredited degree programmes Lead and teach on undergraduate and taught postgraduate Off Campus Division related programmes, leading as appropriate in dedicated areas To contribute and lead, where appropriate, to commercial income generation activity To be responsible for leadership and delivery of teaching, assessment, curriculum development To provide effective academic leadership on the Undergraduate degree Able to successfully and effectively lead and manage academic/research programmes and teams Proven teaching and programme leadership experience including the design, delivery, assessment and validation of modules/courses Able to work individually and under own initiative and to lead and manage projects and motivate others to reach agreed objectives/deadlines
Lecturer in Design Innovation	Leading practical learning activities Leading seminars and other learning activities Leading or contributing to strategic projects and initiatives Recognized as playing a leading international role and being the clear national leader in a number of thematic areas of research A strong record of research, publications, teaching and academic leadership
Programme Manager	Can you shape the business leaders of tomorrow? (this was a headline caption for the job advertisement)
Principal Teaching Fellow	Provide academic leadership Provide leadership to those working within programme areas, as course leader or equivalent
Lecturer in Finance	Provide academic leadership and assume roles of responsibility within the School or the University Provide leadership to more junior academic colleagues within the group and the School as required Prepare articles of world-leading and internationally excellent quality Engage in or lead efforts to attract contract research or consultancy Engage in internationally excellent and/or world-leading research and scholarship, leading research projects

18 Against 'Leadership'

Title of Job	Extracts from person specification and job description
	Provide academic and operational leadership [have] Research leadership & management skills Lead or contribute to the delivery of the following modules … [Experience of] leadership in institutional and/or professional accreditations … leading projects to enhance learning and teaching Evidence of leading and managing a research effort A distinctive contribution to intellectual leadership We expect our senior faculty to be enthusiastic and entrepreneurial research leaders
Lecturer in Digital Marketing (temporary, 12 month contract)	Provide academic leadership through helping to maintain and enhance a research culture Contribute to team effectiveness, leadership/management and administration
Lecturer in Marketing	You will be expected to lead/teach on at least one Marketing module All individuals will make a balanced contribution to teaching and learning and research, and will demonstrate academic leadership Contribute to and/or lead in the development or design of the curriculum and of innovative programmes Exercise academic leadership and supervision in research and teaching as a lecturer, course coordinator and/or mentor to peers, colleagues, and students Providing leadership and support to colleagues within the University, for example as a Module Leader or Programme Leader of a small/medium size programme
Professor of Accounting	Be prepared to lead on external activity, contributing to income streams and the School's standing with industry and international partners Demonstrate senior academic leadership in both teaching and research, and support the management and strategic planning processes of the School and the University Provide academic leadership in the subject area and mentorship for junior academic staff Proven success in academic leadership Willingness to contribute to and lead further development of the Business School.

However, what we would invite you to consider is how leadership is used to describe any of the three dimensions of research, teaching and administration; and it is something expected even in very junior roles. (None of the roles we have included are especially senior in terms of university administration.) Please notice also that in these advertisements 'leadership' is not just being used as a synonym for 'management' or for teaching or research. What you can see in Table 2.3 is that we have 'leadership in academic research' as well as 'academic leadership' which implies that this kind of leading is different from teaching or research leading. Throughout these adverts it is clearly being signalled that leadership is supposed to be something over and above these things and that it is somehow 'good' and 'special'.

When we look at this kind of language, which is ever-present in our sector, it seems simply bizarre. Each and every job here supposedly needs some kind(s) of leadership. Even so, and without being at all unkind to any of our colleagues, we ourselves fail to see any evidence of what might generally be thought of as leadership in our daily work lives.

Academics that we have met and worked with are more or less competent, prolific, talented, conscientious and so on. We have worked for some talented Deans and we have known many people who are high-performers, as well as others who are less than average or prima donnas. However, we have never met anyone in academia that we would want to call a 'leader'. This is because the resonances we associate with the term – for instance the charismatic, vision-creating focus of followers' admiration – simply do not fit. When Immanuel Kant wrote his *Critique of Practical Reason*, the book that revolutionized how we understand ethics, was he 'providing academic leadership'? If not, and we would not describe such a contribution in that way, then how on earth can *we* hope to be doing it? How can someone be expected to be doing it on a twelve-month temporary contract (the basis on which many junior academics are employed these days)?

Staying with the context we know the best, if there were one sector you were looking for 'leaders' in – would it be HE? Be honest, would you look for 'leaders' in the kinds of jobs listed in Table 2.3 – among university lecturers and professors? People who have a talent for academic work have typically done very well in school and in formal education – they tend to be good at solitary activities such as studying, taking exams and writing (or, more accurately perhaps, a particular kind of writing). Without wishing to caricature too much, or to be cruel to colleagues or indeed ourselves, certain kinds of people tend to be very good at exams and at working alone on written documents. They/we are probably not the kind of people who would generally be classified as 'leaders'.

Producing academic work – for most people in the social sciences – is a largely solitary activity. This is true even if collecting research can involve working as a team and it can also involve some very social activities such as talking to people. It is true even if the most creative leaps forward come about as a result of discussions with others. Even when working with other colleagues and co-authors, the writing and analysis that lies at the core of most academic work will often involve working alone. Typically, co-authoring, or – as none of our colleagues would call it – 'team working' means taking it in turns to work on written documents which are then reviewed (anonymously) by other academics.

Again, if you were to stop and imagine this work environment we have sketched, and the kind of person who does well in it, ask yourself – are they likely to be a 'leader'? We would say not; at least in the sense that the cultural caricature of the academic has virtually no overlap whatsoever with a cultural caricature of the leader. We would also say the basic job description and person specification for an academic role has not changed in a way that means we now require more leaders (even though the university context has undoubtedly changed dramatically over the last twenty years). We do not think any more leaders are graduating or that leaders nowadays gravitate towards HE rather than other fields, or that leaders are doing better in exams and so on. Something very strange is happening here it would seem. There is a complete disconnect (for us at least) between the kind of formal and public language that is used to describe the work involved in delivering HE and our lived experience of working in HE.

In response, the people trying to fill these vacancies might argue that whilst it may be true of HE as a whole that it is not blessed or overflowing with leaders, they – for this particular vacancy – are looking for someone exceptional. Well, they would say that wouldn't they? But then these are fairly common or routine jobs in our profession. Moreover, even if we were to imagine for a moment that the job descriptions above were accurate and valid, and we were to imagine further that people were being correctly selected on this basis, then every one of our colleagues – as well as ourselves – would be leaders of some description. In addition, we would be showing leadership on an almost daily basis in a number of different areas of practice (teaching, research, administration). But, and again we need to say this without any disrespect to our colleagues, this strikes us as completely absurd. These jobs and these activities are not 'leadership' in any meaningful sense whatsoever. Leadership is simply being used almost like an aerosol – sprayed over every activity to make it somehow 'special'.

When Is a Leader Not a Leader?

This spread of the language of leadership raises some puzzling questions. For example, when does someone become a leader and when do they stop being a leader? If they are promoted at work to a role which is described as leader do they then also become a leader at home? Or, do they become a leader when they put a suit on, or start their company car, or walk through the door, or when they log on and reply to that first email? If they have one productive phone call followed by another that is not productive are they only showing leadership in that first conversation? If their 3-year-old soils themselves is that no longer an accident but a parent-leadership failure? Does everyone in any organization have 'leadership potential' – even *that* guy (you know the one)? If Barry from accounts, or Glenda from purchasing has to cover a shift while their line manager is away, do they become a 'leader' only to fade back into the ranks when their line manager returns? Or do they only become a leader if they 'show leadership' during that shift?

These are the sorts of questions never answered (indeed never asked) by leadership gurus nor by the vast majority of academics who write about leadership. This is because many academics, almost like football commentators, seem to take these readymade phrases for granted. Even critical scholars who spend some time defining leadership never seem to question whether 'leadership' itself is a good or useful way to describe work relations.

Trouble Defining 'Leadership'

Contemporary writers, whether they are gurus, commentators, business people or academics, rarely make any serious attempt to define 'leadership'. Presumably this is because it is simply assumed that what leadership means is widely understood. This strikes us as very odd given how much diversity there is in how 'leader' or 'leadership' are used (as we showed earlier in the tables of 'leadership failures' and 'strong leadership'). A lot of contemporary research carried out by leadership academics seems to consist of giving senior people (who are already referred to as leaders by the researchers) a questionnaire to complete about some aspect of leadership. As Mats Alvesson and Andre Spicer (2011: 20) argue, this kind of research:

> [I]s based on a set of assumptions and methods that actually produces 'leadership': respondents are thought to be 'leaders' and asked to report about their leadership. Seldom are they asked to consider whether 'leadership' is a relevant term. Even less frequently are they asked to think critically about leadership.

Of course, there are more sophisticated and critical research accounts of leadership available. However, even in these more sophisticated accounts the attempt to define leadership feels short-lived and tokenistic, rather like most people's New Year's resolutions. There is often an initial review and discussion about how problematic the term 'leadership' is, and perhaps an earnest, if rather banal debate about the various ways in which a 'leader' is very different from a 'manager'. Later on in the text though this kind of discussion is, for all intents and purposes, ignored. In effect, 'leader' usually remains a kind of casual synonym for 'boss'.

This kind of practice can occur in surprising places. Take for example, Keith Grint's 2010 book *Leadership: A Very Short Introduction*. Grint's credentials for writing a 126-page introduction to leadership for a non-specialist reader are impeccable. For many years he has written extensively, brilliantly and critically about leadership, having also co-founded the scholarly journal *Leadership*. He tackles the question of defining who is (and is not) a leader, in two ways. His first approach is to say that 'the simplest definition of leadership [is]: having followers' (2010: 2). The other way he seeks to define leadership is against management:

> [M]anagement is the equivalent of *déjà vu* (seen this before), whereas leadership is the equivalent of *vu jàdé* (never seen this before). If this is valid, when acting as a manager, you are required to engage the requisite process – the standard operating procedure (SOP) to resolve the previously experienced problem the last time it emerged. In contrast, when you are acting as a leader, you are required to facilitate the construction of an innovative response to the novel or recalcitrant problem. Management and leadership ... [are therefore] two forms of authority rooted in the distinction between certainty and uncertainty (2010: 15).

Both of these definitions have a long pedigree in different traditions within leadership research, and we think that both can be useful when used judiciously (in fact, we have already used 'having followers' in the first few pages of this book). Nevertheless these definitions still have problems. For example, the first definition – a leader is someone who has followers – is not only somewhat hollow it also simply passes on the problem of definition. The next question becomes: 'how do you define a follower?' As we discuss in more detail in Chapter 9, Grint's book never defines a follower.

One difficulty with the second definition is that the apparently neat distinction between certainty and uncertainty seems likely to be messier than Grint implies. For example, who gets to define certainty or uncertainty? From the outside, it is often impossible to tell whether someone is dealing with certainty or uncertainty just by looking at the nature of the task or situation. Partly because managers are comparatively powerful, they very often have the choice themselves of how they think about their work. Some will think that what most of us would see as a highly complex task or situation is a matter of certainty, others approaching the same task or situation would see it as a matter of uncertainty. Indeed – whatever they might actually be doing – a manager using this description could claim they are always dealing with uncertainty of some kind. Perhaps they are always thinking about 'role-modelling leadership' or being a 'servant leader' even when doing mundane tasks. This kind of re-imagining of work and identity must be commonplace because thinking of oneself as a leader has become a much more prestigious and positive way to narrate one's life and work. It so obviously trumps thinking of oneself as dealing with standard operating procedures for instance. Even if someone is only a leader some of the time, Grint's description implies the same individual could veer between being a leader and a manager as they go from task to task, minute to minute. It leaves us with some of the puzzling questions we discussed earlier – about when exactly someone becomes a leader.

There is a larger point to be made here though. In contrast to many other leadership scholars, Grint is initially much more careful and thoughtful. He is asserting explicitly that senior people with formal authority over others in organizations are not necessarily, or automatically leaders. Indeed, from the definitions he offers, readers might well form the view that 'real' leaders (i.e. people fitting both these definitions) are rare. In practice though, throughout the rest of his book, Grint appears to go back on his own definitions. For instance, he uses 'leader' and 'follower' in precisely the same situations where 'manager' and 'worker' would have been the more traditional terms. This is despite his description of the leader as a figure who is almost opposed to the manager in their grappling with uncertainty. For instance, among countless other similar examples, we read that:

> [I]t is the assiduous leaders who ... consistently ask about the health of their followers' families, or who always make a point of ensuring their followers are in agreement with the direction of the organization and their work rate, who build the networks that make the organization work (2010: 13).

It would seem odd to assume this advice to 'assiduous leaders' applies only to *leaders* (i.e. those who 'facilitate the construction of an innovative response to the novel or recalcitrant problem') and not to *managers* (those who are merely engaging 'standard operating procedures'). It seems equally odd to suggest bosses are only able to ask consistently about the health of their subordinates' families if they knew these subordinates are their *followers*. Asking after colleagues' families seems to be something even the least powerful supervisor could do. It does not seem complex or strategic, or anything to do with uncertainty or any difference between leaders and managers. Presumably, whether or not we are a leader – or someone is our follower – it is a good thing to do.

In another sign of 'leader' being used very generally, the section in Grint's book on 'modern leadership studies' (pp. 40–45) discusses work that is generally found in textbooks on management. Maslow's hierarchy of needs, for example, is said to argue 'that leaders need to sort out their followers' health and safety before the followers will focus on "higher needs"' (2010: 43). But Maslow used neither 'leader' nor 'follower' in his analyses. Neither did F. W. Taylor (the author of *Scientific Management*), whose work is nevertheless read as being primarily about leadership. Grint tells us that under Taylor: 'leadership was reconfigured as "knowledge leadership" with the leaders as repositories of knowledge' (2010: 41).

On the book's last page Grint also appears to go explicitly against his foundational definitions – which contrast management with leadership – in a somewhat different way. His concluding claim is that all organizations (other than small scale or temporary networks) 'seem to require some form of institutionalized leadership' (2010: 126). But, using his earlier definitions which imply leadership is a rarity, there must be many organizations which only ever have managers not leaders. Similarly, it is possible for organizations to exist where people comply and cooperate but do not really 'follow' others in any meaningful way. This, using Grint's first definition, rules out the existence of leadership in that organization.

What should we make of these apparent inconsistencies? One possibility is to assume that when Grint writes 'leader' and 'follower' he is making empirical claims. In other words, he is suggesting that most senior people spend most of their time on activities that count as leadership (rather than management) and that most subordinates generally follow executives (rather than just accepting their authority). The problem with this reading is that he doesn't offer any evidence or argument in favour of that position. Another possibility is that the introductory distinctions between management and leadership are largely ceremonial. Like the token New Year's resolution, we may be disappointed when it evaporates, but perhaps we are also not that surprised. This reading suggests these distinctions simply establish that Grint is writing about leadership, which, as we show in Chapter 10 is a genre with its own distinctive conventions. One convention of the genre, unsurprisingly, is that leadership authors use the terms 'leader' (and 'follower') a lot.

Leaders as Elites

In the light of these definitional debates, let us now turn to look at how the terms 'leadership' and 'leaders' are commonly used in the corporate sector and other work organizations, both public and private. What seems to have happened here is that the generic 'anything-that-is-good-about-someone' equals leadership (i.e. what we see emerging in press reports, football commentary, schools, academia etc.) is used. At the same time however, this very generic way of talking about leadership has been fused with ideas from formal definitions like those we have seen offered by Grint. These latter definitions imply that leadership remains a high-prestige activity, only carried out by bosses. In its corporate usage therefore 'leaders' can (in theory) be anyone. In practice, however, the people referred to as 'leaders' are invariably bosses; but because they are 'leaders' they tend to be imagined (at least by themselves and their peers) as particular kinds of bosses.

For example, even though as we have seen, in higher education almost everyone is expected to show leadership, still, the term 'leader' is also applied specifically to high-status individuals. It is as if more junior people should 'show leadership' etc. in order to try to mimic idealized senior staff. Today, as we write, the latest issue of the trade paper for UK academics – *The Times Higher Education* – ran a full-page advert headed:

LEADERSHIP SUMMIT:
WISDOM, GRIT & COMPASSION

The **Leadership Summit** has become a key event for leaders in higher education and participants will leave with the latest thinking on why **wisdom, grit and compassion** are core essentials that underpin all leadership, how the sector is changing, and what it means to be a leader today in a complex environment. Our keynote speaker and author of best-selling business book, *The Naked Leader*, David Taylor will be joined by a great line up of leaders and contributors (*The Times Higher Education*, 24th – 30th May 2018: 4; bold in original)

The 'leaders' for whom this occasion has apparently become a key event are clearly meant to be top people. Similarly the 'great line up of leaders' who are the speakers all appear to be vice-chancellors (equivalent to university presidents in the US) or people with similarly high-status roles. In any event, we can be pretty certain that neither the speakers nor the 'leaders' at whom the event is aimed are the ordinary lecturers on temporary contracts who, as we saw earlier in this chapter, are still also expected somehow to 'show leadership'.

In most organizations nowadays, *all* elites are imagined to be leaders. This kind of imagining is what makes so many large companies hardly bat an eyelid before spending huge sums of money to develop their so-called leaders (i.e. their top people). Perhaps not entirely coincidentally, when it comes to the study of business and management, it is hard to think of a bigger growth industry than leadership – especially over the last couple of decades. Unsurprisingly enough, almost all leadership research is concentrated on elites. In fact, leadership has become something of an obsession for many in contemporary organizational life – the focus of a great deal of corporate training and consultancy not to mention popular management books. Thousands of books and articles have been written on what makes someone a leader, how to be a leader (or how to exercise leadership), what kind of leader to be (what leadership style to learn and adopt) and so on. In almost all these books and articles 'leadership' is clearly being used in the sense of carrying out a formal, elite role. These various texts and practices make up what is often called the leadership industry and if you have read this far into the book then you are likely to be as interested in the leadership industry as we are. (Even this phrase, the 'leadership industry' is dripping with the insidious and unchallenged values of neo-liberalism: that every entity and every concept can and should be commodified and consumed.)

Today's Senior Leadership Team; Yesterday's Senior Management Team

This slippage between leader and manager is certainly not confined to academics. As we mentioned in the introduction, the ways in which we use the language of leadership have shifted quite profoundly. Of course, the changes have happened very gradually and informally so that we may have hardly noticed them, and there will always be exceptions to the rule. But many organizations which have a 'senior leadership team' today had exactly the same group a few years ago, only called a 'senior management team'. Similarly, it is very difficult to go on a 'management development' course nowadays; just as, a generation ago, it would have been virtually impossible to go on a 'leadership development' course. Our point is that the names have changed – even if they are essentially the same courses.

What, then, are we to make of the practice of relabelling things 'leadership' that were formerly known as management? It is, on the face of it, as we have already said, a very odd practice – albeit a common one. Indeed, there is something strangely self-defeating about it. Of those writers who make any effort to define 'leadership', they almost invariably do so by drawing a contrast between 'leadership' and 'management'. For example: managers are transactional, leaders are transformational; managers get people to work to contract, leaders get people to go beyond contract; managers get people to comply, leaders get people to follow and so on. As we have seen, this sort of distinction is exactly what Grint does in his own definition.

Joseph Rost in his influential book, *Leadership for the Twenty-First Century*, sets out this position particularly unambiguously. His views are worth citing at some length:

> Leaders are not the same as managers. Followers are not the same as subordinates. Managers may be leaders, but if they are leaders, they are involved in a relationship different from management. Subordinates may be followers, but if they are followers, they are involved in a relationship different from management. Leaders need not be managers to be leaders. Followers need not be subordinates to be followers. People in authority positions – presidents, governors, mayors, CEOs, superintendents, principals, administrators, supervisors, departmental heads, and so on – are not automatically leaders by virtue of their holding a position of authority. Being a leader must not be equated with being in a position of authority. The definition of a leader cannot include a requirement that the person be in a position of authority ... On the other hand, people in authority positions are automatically managers because that is the definition of a manager: a person who holds a positon of authority. ... A distinction between leadership and management requires that the words *leader* and *manager, follower* and *subordinate*, be defined differently. The two sets of words cannot be used interchangeably (Rost, 1991: 150–51; italics in original).

Now, Rost would surely be on the right lines if 'leadership' were to mean anything more than just a more glamourous-sounding synonym for 'management'. Definitions like his would doubtless be widely accepted by many of those in the 'leadership industry'. However, as we have already shown to an extent, when we look at how the language of leadership is *actually* used, these distinctions between leadership and management almost always disappear. Indeed, we would go so far as to claim that in the vast majority of cases, whenever we see 'leader' or 'leadership' at work we can just cross the word out and replace it with 'manager' or 'management', with no loss of semantic meaning.

Needless to say, simply relabelling a job that used to be a 'management role', as a 'leadership role', has no credible intellectual basis, but there is something very odd happening here. What happens in practice goes explicitly against the whole point of the work that Rost is trying to do. As Grint does, he is deliberately, and with emphasis, defining 'leadership' as something distinctively different ('special', 'good' and 'successful' in some way) from 'management'. But is there anything more to these definitional projects than interest-serving ceremony?

3

MEASURING THE LANGUAGE OF LEADERSHIP

We shall return to whose interests the language of leadership supports in Chapter 4. Before we do so however, we want to provide more evidence that the way the language of leadership is being used has in fact changed significantly over the last few years. Further evidence is ideally required even though we suspect that many readers, especially those who have worked in organizations for more than a few years, will already recognize how the language of leadership is replacing (or possibly has replaced) the language of management in their own organization. The good news, from our point of view at least, is that changes in the ways we use the language of leadership can be measured, at least to some extent.

To do so, we have analyzed databases of ordinary language using an approach called 'corpus linguistics' (we are indebted to Gerlinde Mautner for her help introducing us to this set of techniques). A corpus simply means a body of text; linguistics is the systematic study of language. One commonly used database of ordinary language is the British National Corpus (BNC). The BNC is a '100 million word collection of samples of written and spoken language from a wide range of sources, designed to represent a wide cross-section of British English, both spoken and written, from the late twentieth century' (BNC, 2017). The 'late twentieth century' means the early 1990s, roughly speaking – as we shall see when we look at some actual examples of the words it uses. More recently, a new corpus of some 15 billion words has become available, called the English Web 2015 (enTenTen15). It uses words from similar sources, only now looking at words used during 2015 – some twenty-five years later.

The two corpora (the plural of *corpus*) i.e. the BNC and the English Web 2015 (enTenTen15) are designed somewhat differently and are of different sizes. We use them together in order to obtain a picture of the changes that have occurred in the language of leadership. However, because of the nature of the corpora involved it is not possible to make highly precise or definitive claims – rather we use them to point to broad trends. We should also emphasize that what we are using are corpora that contain specifically British English material. We have been careful, therefore, not to claim anything about what might (or might not) be going on in other English-speaking countries (such as the USA, for example).

With these caveats, these two corpora represent a rich source for understanding what is happening when people use certain terms – and, broadly speaking, how the use has changed over time. To analyze the two corpora we used a specially designed software programme called Sketchengine (Sketchengine, 2017). It allows us not only to count the occurrences of words but also (among many other things) to examine the contexts in which words occur and on that basis build what are called 'collocational profiles' (Mautner, 2005). Collocation is when words occur near one another in a text; in a sense this is when they are semantic neighbours. It can be instructive to study collocation because we can start to learn how different terms are interrelated. As Irene Pollach (2012: 207) argues:

> Collocations can become carriers of cultural meanings or domain-specific meanings ... A collocation analysis therefore reveals ... patterns and meanings that are evident neither from frequency lists of individual words, nor from the readings of larger volumes of text in a manual analysis.

We return to these corpora and collocation to examine the words 'worker' and 'follower' in Chapter 9.

New Leaders?

We have used Sketchengine to construct Table 3.1. It shows part of a 'word sketch' of the term 'leader'. A word sketch is the operation performed by Sketchengine software that provides a summary of the word's collocational behaviour. Table 3.1 ranks the commonest collocated words that modified 'leader' in the early 1990s and sets these results against the equivalent collocations in 2015. So, for example, in the early 1990s, the word that was most commonly placed before 'leader' to describe (or modify) it was 'party' (i.e. 'party leader'). However, in 2015 the commonest modifier was 'team' (i.e. 'team leader').

Table 3.1 shows clearly that there have been some profound shifts in the way that the term 'leader' was used in day-to-day language in the early 1990s in Britain as compared to 2015. For example, in the earlier period, the dominant way 'leader' was used was to refer to political activities: the top six collocations all clearly refer to political issues (broadly defined), as do the majority of the other collocations in the entire list of twenty-two.

Another big change between the two periods is apparent in the organizationally relevant uses of 'leader'. Organizationally relevant uses are strikingly more common in 2015 as compared to the early 1990s. In the early 1990s, though 'team leader' is in

TABLE 3.1 Word Sketch of the Use of 'Leader' in the Early 1990s and 2015: Commonest Modifier of 'Leader'

	Early 1990s	2015
1	Party	Team
2	Union	Community
3	Opposition	Industry
4	Deputy	Business
5	Labour	Religious
6	Soviet	World
7	Team	Church
8	Church	Political
9	Former	Global
10	Political	Group
11	Project	Party
12	World	Senior
13	Market	Union
14	Religious	Future
15	Spiritual	Market
16	Trade	Thought
17	Military	Project
18	Group	Youth
19	Communist	Opposition
20	Democratic	Local
21	Community	National
22	Business	Woman

7th place, we have to go all the way down to 22nd place before we find 'business leader'. Arguably, 'project leader' (11th) and 'group leader' (18th) may also be relevant to corporate life; though if so, the use of such terms seems likely to be relatively common in other settings too. In the early 1990s, therefore, we can be pretty sure that 'leader' was predominantly used to describe senior politicians.

In comparison, looking at 2015, while the use of 'leader' for politicians and political roles more generally is still present, it is less prominent. At the same time, terms related directly to organizational life have become *much* commoner. In fact, the term 'team' has become the commonest modifier of 'leader' with 'industry leader' in third place (a term that was not even in the list in the 1990s) and 'business leader' now up from 22nd to 4th. Interestingly, 'senior leader' (a term that did not appear in the top twenty-two in the early 1990s) is in 12th place by 2015.

The common occurrence of 'senior leader' strikes us as particularly interesting in the light of our arguments about how the term leader is actually used in organizational settings. This is because the term 'senior leader' suggests that by 2015 it had become relatively commonplace to talk about leaders in the context of organizational hierarchies. This is in spite of the fact that, as we saw in the last chapter, many leadership writers try to insist that whether one counts as a leader or not should have nothing to do with hierarchies or seniority as such. The occurrence of 'senior leader' in the latest list of commonly used modifiers (along with its absence from the earlier one) directly supports the view that 'leader' is starting to replace 'manager' as something like a synonym. This is because it does not make much sense to talk about leaders as 'senior' if, in essence, leaders are people who others follow – regardless of their hierarchical position – as we have seen both Rost and Grint seem to suggest. It does make perfect sense, however, to talk about senior managers. This is because a manager is, by definition, someone with a place in an organizational hierarchy. After all, is there ever going to be a 'senior leader' in the context of organizational life who we could not equally call a 'manager'? So, let us now turn to Table 3.2 and the same word sketch; this time for the term 'manager'.

TABLE 3.2 Word Sketch of the Use of 'Manager' in the Early 1990s and 2015: Commonest Modifier of 'Manager'

	Early 1990s	2015
1	Senior	Project
2	Bank	General
3	Lifespan	Program
4	Fund	Senior
5	General	General
6	Project	Case
7	Marketing	Marketing
8	Assistant	Fund
9	Sale	Product
10	Line	Account
11	Team	Senior
12	General	Operations
13	Branch	Sale
14	England	Development
15	Business	Business
16	Area	Office
17	Service	Assistant
18	Care	Programme
19	Group	Resource
20	Lan	City
21	Corporate	Property
22	Middle	Manager

Same Old Managers?

Clearly, there have been some changes in the use of the term manager over the same period. Bank managers are perhaps an unsurprising omission from the 2015 list, though the term 'bank' was the second commonest modifier of 'manager' in the early 1990s. Overall though, almost all the commonest collocations are work- or business-related with nothing in any way comparable to the striking changes that have been associated with the word 'leader'.

Of course, the meanings and associations of individual words change over time. For example, it seems likely that the rise of social media has significantly changed the way we use words. There is nothing inherently sinister or worrying about these kinds of changes as such. Nevertheless, the apparently profound shift from manager to leader is still striking. Especially as it seems to have occurred in the relatively short period of twenty-five years; and particularly because 'leader' is such a prestigious word – linked as it is to world leaders and other top politicians.

We cannot legitimately make too much in the way of firm conclusions about this shift. Nevertheless, our findings provide an interesting and suggestive jumping off point for the rest of the book. Furthermore, our data are in line with what we already know from small-scale studies conducted in organization studies specifically. For example, Dermot O'Reilly and Mike Reed (2010: 963) found a dramatic shift in the language used within UK government policy documents: 'the ratio of the total of UK government public administration documents containing the keyword "leadership" for the period of the Labour government [1997–2010] compared to the previous Conservative government [1988–1997] is of the order of 11:1.' Similarly, Keith Grint et al (2017: 3) record that while in 2003 'there were 14,139 items relating to "leadership" on Amazon.co.uk for sale … [by] January 2015 there were 126,149 items.'

We can also find examples of how the slippage from manager to leader is now part of popular culture. For instance, in series 11, episode 1 of the highly successful TV science fiction series *Dr Who*, 'The Woman Who Fell to Earth' (first broadcast by the BBC on 7th October 2018) the Doctor encounters an alien life-form called Zim Sha. When Sha claims that he is 'soon-to-be leader of the Stenza warrior race, conquerors of the nine systems' the Doctor quips back at him: 'When you say, "soon-to-be-leader," what are you now? The office junior?' (Text available at The Woman Who Fell to Earth, 2018.) It is interesting that by 2018, even in a TV show aimed primarily at children, it has become possible to make a joke out of the slippage in the changing connotations of the term 'leader'. The term is no longer understood simply as a political or quasi-political figure (in Sha's case, the 'leader of the Stenza warrior race'). In the workplace it has also become the opposite of 'office junior'; which is to say that 'leader' is now widely understood to refer to a senior work role; a work role that must surely be something very similar to a manager if its antithesis is office junior.

4

POLISHING OUR CHAINS

Having established that many of us are indeed using the language of leadership much more commonly than we used to, we now look in more detail at why it matters that we are doing so. Chapter 1 summarizes our concerns about two aspects to the language of leadership: (i) flattering bosses and (ii) flattening workers. As an initial illustration of why it matters whether we use the language of leadership – or whether we use alternatives such as 'managers' and 'workers' – consider Table 4.1. In the right-hand column is a short extract from the recent writings of another eminent critical leadership scholar – David Collinson. In the left-hand column is some work Collinson published twenty-six years earlier.

One thing that is interesting about Collinson's work is that it seems to parallel the changes in use of ordinary language over the same period we just analyzed using corpus linguistics. In the 1988 article, his natural categories of analysis seemed to be 'manager' and 'worker'. In fact he never mentions the term leader in 1988 at all. In the 2014 article though, while he does still refer to 'managers' and 'workers' on occasion in other parts of the article, he now seems strongly to prefer 'leader' and 'follower'. These are terms that he seems to be using routinely and contrary to both Grint and Rost who appear to insist that 'leader' and 'manager' are necessarily different.

Depoliticizing the Workplace

The first thing that strikes us about this table is just how radically Collinson has chosen to re-present his earlier work in the language of the leader-follower. We say re-present because, as mentioned, throughout his 1988 paper he used neither term (leader nor follower); yet when he refers to his earlier work in the 2014 paper he says he was talking about leaders. In other words, it seems pretty clear that in 2014 he uses 'leader' and 'follower' in the same way as he used 'manager' and 'worker' in 1988.

34 Against 'Leadership'

TABLE 4.1 From Shop-Floor Worker to Follower; From 'The Management' to Leaders

Collinson (1988: 186–7)	Collinson (2014: 44)
Shop-floor humour directed at managers was usually concerned to negate and distance them … By contrast, management repeatedly sought to engage shop stewards in humorous interaction. Yet, the stewards were aware that this managerial humour was intended to obscure conflict behind personalized relations, which tried to deny the hierarchical structure of status and power … Six years earlier the company had been taken over by an American multi-national … As part of the American's campaign to win the trust of the workforce, a company in-house magazine was introduced. The paper was dismissed widely as a 'Let's be pals act' and nicknamed … 'Goebbel's Gazette.' … The intention of managerial humour [included in the Gazette], to reduce conflict and emphasize organizational harmony, had the opposite effect of merely reinforcing the polarization between management and shop-floor.	My own research in organizations over the past 30 years has found a recurrent … pattern. This is for organizational leaders to be either unaware of organizational tensions and paradoxes or, if they are informed of them, to try to deny or downplay their nature, extent, and consequences. This is especially the case with regard to leaders' relations with followers/employees. Leaders' hierarchical position 'at the top' of organizations can result in them being distant and detached from 'the front line' where many of the organization's tensions are often most acutely experienced … Equally, followers may face considerable difficulties and barriers in seeking to voice their 'critical upward communication' to those in senior positions … Consequently, leaders can be largely unaware of fundamental tensions and contradictions embedded within routine organizational practices.

What this change does, at least in our view, is depoliticize the workplace and indeed depoliticize Collinson's own work. Collinson (2017) himself has disagreed with us on this point, but see if you agree. Looking at the 1988 piece first, this has the feel of a radical critique of 'management' as voiced from the perspective of the shop-floor. In the 2014 extract, there is a more conciliatory, manager-orientated (or rather we should say 'leader-orientated') tone. It is as if the 2014 version were addressed primarily to and written for so-called 'leaders'. What is more, these 'leaders' seem to be equated with elites; in the same way as 'managers' were equated with elites in the 1988 piece. It is still critical in the sense that it says mildly uncomfortable things about those elites, but these are more mildly critical – i.e. that they can be out of touch, unaware or unsympathetic. But where is all the Marxian-inflected rhetoric from the 1988 extract (e.g. 'obscure conflict'; 'hierarchical structure of status and power'; 'the polarization between management and shop-floor', etc.)? By 2014 it has seemingly disappeared.

To us, these changes have the effect of significantly depoliticizing the 2014 account when compared to the 1988 paper. The use of terms like 'leader' and 'follower' make the critique less challenging to the powerful, with no sense of workers' voices coming through. In other words, the use of the term 'leader', compared to 'manager' both glamourizes the role of bosses while at the same time encouraging us to turn our eyes away from the less wholesome things done by these 'leaders'. This supports our concern that this readymade language of leadership leads to flattering of bosses and flattening of workers.

Collinson's work is also interesting for what it tells us about swapping 'follower' for shop-floor 'worker'. Being a 'follower' seems so unlikely to be part of what Collinson (1988: 185) himself calls the 'cultural identities' of most ordinary workers across the world. Even if you have not read his 1988 paper (which we would highly recommend you do), you could perhaps tell this simply from the nicknames Collinson says these shop-floor workers had. He calls people 'Fat Rat', 'Bastard Jack', 'Big Lemon' and 'The Snake'. Is it likely *they* thought of their identity using the term 'follower'? Surely not!

TGI Fridays

We can imagine quite a few readers will doubt that academic writing matters much – whatever it might say. While we (as academics) would disagree, it is important even so to provide a parallel illustration of why the language of leadership matters – this time from the 'real world' of a commercial organization. Below, then, is a letter from Lauren, one of 'TGI Fridays workers' addressed to Karen Forrester, the company's CEO in the UK. As we write, the letter is being widely circulated on social media to back a strike campaign. In contrast to most TGI Fridays workers, Ms. Forrester's own salary as CEO is significantly above the UK government's national living wage rate that Lauren's letter mentions. You may not be surprised to hear that the figure given in the public domain for her pay is well over £1 million per year. Here is Lauren's letter to Karen:

> From: TGI Fridays Workers
>
> We have worked for you for five, ten, fifteen or even twenty years. We stayed. We were loyal. Made careers out of waitressing and bartending, a rare phenomenon within the UK restaurant industry, which tends to have high staff turnover rates.
>
> We trained hard to be the best in the business, we certified and re-certified, even when you made us download the 'TGI Fridays Academy' app and complete our training at home, off the clock and unpaid.
>
> When you took time and a half away from us on bank holidays, and then away from us over Christmas Eve and New Year, we didn't kick up much of a fuss.
>
> When stores began to lose shift meals, meaning we now work 12 hour shifts and have to pay to eat food that we know costs the company a fraction of the price we're forced to pay, we started to question what was happening to our beloved Fridays.
>
> Then in January it hit us. Every time the government's national living wage increased TGI Fridays would try to claw that money back by stripping away our perks and benefits.
>
> When early in the new year and with just two days' notice you told us you told us that you were taking 40% of waiting staffs' card tips and giving them to the kitchen, we'd had enough.

The 33p per hour national minimum wage increase set by the government that we had been so excited for was wiped out in an instant, and we instead found ourselves heading into the new year facing financial losses of £250 a month because of this cruel tip policy change.

To add insult to injury, you gave us just two days' notice to figure out how we were going to pay our mortgages, buy our weekly groceries or carry on paying for our children's extracurricular activities.

We wanted answers – but when we called the phone number provided to us you didn't answer.

You claim to have an open door policy but when we sought answers to our questions we have been repeatedly shut down.

A few years ago the kitchen were paid a much higher hourly rate than front of house, but as the minimum wage has increased chefs' wages have stayed the same.

You should have been increasing their pay in line with living costs year on year, that would have been the right thing to do. Instead you have taken from front of house staff, many who already live paycheque to paycheque.

You claim that 'servers still keep 100% of their cash tips.' This is a lie. You know that your waiters and waitresses already take a percentage from their total tips and share them. This money is given to the bartender who made the drinks, the server assistants who laid the tables and ran the food, and the guys who take our guests their desserts.

This isn't about minimum wage servers not wanting to share. It's about a company whose shareholders have gotten so greedy that they no longer want to pay their hardworking staff anything above the bare minimum.

All we want is to be heard, and to have our questions answered.

We are not the enemy. We are the faces of Fridays. We love our stores and our teams and our guests. You have lied and denied us access to remedy.

Lauren.

(See: https://campaign.goingtowork.org.uk/petitions/tgi-friday-s-pay-us-fairly?source=twitter-share-email-button&time=1526600348 [Accessed 18th May 2018]).

This is a tale alleging how a boss not only coerces and lies to her workforce, but arbitrarily cuts their wages with a couple of days' notice. We have no insider-knowledge one way or another whether the claims are 'true'. We are simply reproducing something which is in the public domain to make a point about how Lauren uses language. Unsurprisingly, there is no mentions of words like 'leader' or 'follower' in her letter; it would be incongruous, to say the least, if there were. It is surely unimaginable, for example for the letter to have been headed 'From: TGI Fridays Followers'; equally unimaginable for the CEO to be addressed in her letter as Lauren's 'leader'.

Much easier to imagine, however, are the official representations of the UK Company on their own web pages. Unsurprisingly enough, they are starkly different in tone from what we read in Lauren's letter. For instance, the section of the corporate website headed 'Leadership' reads as follows:

> **Leadership**
>
> Karen Forrester, TGI Fridays UK Managing Director, is much loved, valued and respected throughout the company. She is regularly seen in the stores and will always take time with the team. This is also true of the company's new open stores, where Karen and her Exec team take a day to spend with the new Fridays family members to welcome them to the brand. If a key message needs to be delivered to the team, Karen will create a video message which will then be posted onto TGI Fridays social website, and a link is sent directly to their mobile phones (TGI Fridays, 2018).

Conflict situations like the one at TGI Fridays patently make a nonsense out of the routine use of the term 'leader' for senior people – as much as it makes a nonsense out of the routine use of 'follower' for the rank-and-file. These conflict situations are commonplace of course, though they are often downplayed by the media; and most leadership researchers are generally too polite to mention anything like them either (though the work of David Collinson, we are happy to acknowledge, is a notable exception to this rule).

We suggest that the politeness of the overwhelming majority of leadership commentators is, in part, a product of their use of the language of leadership. With all its positive cultural associations, to talk about 'leadership' is inherently to take the side of elites. It downplays, indeed it arguably writes out altogether, the hostile workplace realities faced by people like Lauren and many, many others like her across the world. At the same time, because of the term's strong association with the positive goodness of leaders and their non-coercive influence, when we call bosses 'leaders' doing so also predisposes us to see them in the kind of way that corporations would like us to see their executives. In the case of TGI Fridays, that would be as 'much loved, valued and respected throughout the company'.

The Dominant Image of the Leader

When we speak of 'leaders' doing so implies that a common purpose is shared between the leader and their followers (there are other associations relevant to this debate, which we turn to later in the book.) As we saw in Chapter 2, Keith Grint sums up this dominant association succinctly when he says that the simplest definition of leadership is, 'having followers' (Grint, 2010: 2). Common purpose implies there is something 'good' or 'nice' – and non-coercive – about the work relationships leaders have. This is especially so when leadership is opposed to more traditional ideas about authority in organizations like 'management'.

'Management' has the sorts of cultural associations which, in contrast to leadership, might conjure up images of diverging interests, division, strife and the need for control in workplaces. This is one of the reasons that 'manager' and 'follower' do not tend to go together in normal use.

Just how realistic is it that so-called 'leadership' at work is not coercive at all though? We can readily believe that shared purpose is commonplace, even necessary, in other contexts that have had people called leaders in them for a much longer time than work organizations. Take jazz bands and orchestras, for example; or religious groups. As we saw with the corpus linguistics analysis in Chapter 3, 'leaders' have also been familiar in political parties and trade unions for many years.

In the case of a jazz band (and without wishing to romanticize the life of professional musicians) it seems reasonable to assume that someone like Duke Ellington was said to be the 'leader' of his band because the other musicians respected his outstanding abilities. (Though making sure he paid them regularly – and well above the market rate – also helped to keep them in his band.) In any case, Duke Ellington surely had followers among his fellow musicians in a way that was meaningful. In other words, calling someone in a position like his the 'band leader' is unlikely to be airbrushing out the divergent interests and potential for conflict that the term 'leader' often has in an organizational setting. This is because many people did actually 'follow' him. Similarly, as Kevin has argued, people such as political leaders are typically elected by members of their party and can generally be removed by them if they fail to live up to expectations (Morrell and Hartley, 2006). Of course, we are not saying politics is free from conflict! But if (in a democracy at least) political leaders don't have followers – in the sense of people willing to support and vote for them – then they won't be leaders, or at least not for long. Again, we think it makes sense in terms of Grint's definition 'having followers' to call people like senior politicians 'leaders'.

It seems most unlikely however that we can say the same sorts of things about the overwhelming majority of the people who nowadays get called 'leaders' in ordinary work settings; i.e. the bosses. For a start, while there is literature about anarchistic and other non-hierarchical workplaces (e.g. *ephemera*, 2014), the vast majority of workplaces – i.e. standard corporations and public sector workplaces – have no meaningful democracy. Bosses in workplaces are virtually never like political leaders whom workers can vote out of office if they do not like them. Indeed, few of us get any real say at all about who our boss is going to be. These are hardly the ideal conditions for Grint's 'having followers' definition to be satisfied. Equally, most of us probably have far lower opinions of our boss (to say the least) than members of Duke Ellington's band did about him.

It is commonplace, as we have already pointed out, for workers to be indifferent to their bosses, or even for them often to actively despise them. How, then, can it make sense to regard the average worker as a 'follower'? If we were to do a straw poll asking how many people would happily think of themselves specifically as 'followers' of their boss at work, the answer would surely be very few of us. Furthermore, leaving aside social media (with its proliferation of 'followers') and academic articles about leadership, the term 'follower' actually occurs very rarely in organizational life. As we shall see in Chapter 9, the word 'follower' is only commonly used in everyday language in religious contexts (to mean something very similar to 'disciple').

Perhaps the most basic reason then, why we are against routinely calling organizational elites 'leaders' (and what they do 'leadership') is a straightforward one: we are against it because, almost certainly, the vast majority of bosses are *not* leaders. Or, more precisely, they are not leaders in any kind of meaningful sense of the word – one that doesn't end up being, in effect, an (albeit glamourizing and muddying) synonym for 'boss' or 'manager'.

Calling the people in charge of organizations by their traditional names: things like 'bosses', 'managers', 'CEOs', 'board members', 'executives', 'senior executives', 'head teachers', etc. does make sense to us. These kinds of terms simply describe job roles. What is more, using these terms implies nothing about the relationship these people have with their subordinates. Even if you hate your boss or your manager, she is still your boss. The thing that is different in talking about a 'leader' is that, by definition, subordinates have to enjoy something like non-coercive relationships with them.

We do not wish to be misunderstood here. We are not saying that non-coercive relationships cannot or never exist in organizational life. We recognize and indeed we want to celebrate the fact that, as James MacGregor Burns puts it in his classic book *Leadership* 'not all human influences are necessarily coercive and exploitative' (Burns, 1978/2010: 11). In a particular workplace, where we ourselves thought that non-coercive relationships were the norm (perhaps a truly democratic organization – some of which do exist – see Griffin et al, 2015a), then we think it might well make sense to refer to the person in charge of that workplace as the leader. That said, both of us have worked in a wide variety of jobs and organizations, and although we may have respected our boss (sometimes) we have never yet been inclined to call any of them our leader. We suspect that we are far from alone in this.

The Camouflage of 'Leadership'

The reason all this matters is that the word 'leader' is never *merely* a synonym for 'boss'. Even when 'leader' gets used more or less routinely and unthinkingly in corporate reports and research papers – apparently as a more flattering or euphemistic alternative for 'manager' – it still has significant effects. These effects are importantly different from those that would have occurred had a term like 'CEO' or 'manager' or 'executive' been used instead of 'leader' in the same context.

For instance, many people who would never have considered doing a 'management' job will much more happily take on a role that is called a 'leadership' role. It can feel good to be called a leader, and to be able to think of oneself in that way. Being a manager, on the other hand, tends to make you sound like a bureaucrat, or in league with market capitalism. Nevertheless, as others have pointed out before us, when you try and observe what someone called a leader actually does on a day-to-day basis in their job it is usually impossible to distinguish their work from that of someone who still languishes under the title of a mere manager.

The real trouble is that the people called leaders make exactly the same cuts (or 'efficiency savings') that the people called 'managers' would have traditionally made. This means that the growing trend to call people like senior doctors and nurses, teachers and university academics 'leaders' has had troubling effects. It has meant that the very people who could have traditionally been relied upon to resist commercialization – and would never have been comfortable being called a manager – are nowadays more easily incorporated into the brave new world of competition and markets: simply by being called a 'leader' (see for example, Mathilde Berghout et al's (2018) recent analysis of how framing doctors as 'leaders' is radically reconfiguring the nature of medical professionalism).

Another effect of talking about bosses so positively – as leaders – seems to have been to encourage us to turn our eyes away from the wider injustices many of these so-called leaders have perpetrated. One of the huge ironies of the growth in the popularity of the term 'leader' over the last thirty years or so is that it has occurred at the same time as there has been a massive deterioration in pay, job security and working conditions for many ordinary workers. This is the sort of deterioration that hardly suggests happy relations between the so-called leaders and their supposed followers – not least because it has directly benefited senior staff at the expense of ordinary workers.

We say that it is an irony; but actually the deterioration in working conditions for ordinary workers can be seen as part of what the language of leadership actively facilitates. After all, if you are a leader (rather than a mere manager) then your status as a leader suggests that you should expect to be admired, that you believe that you should merit a larger salary, that you deserve to be made to feel special – and so on. All these things rely, at least in part, on ensuring others have less of what is deemed desirable, relatively speaking. Furthermore, because 'leader' has connotations of rightful supremacy it provides justification or cover for the 'tough decisions' in which the deterioration of workers' rights and conditions is simultaneously evidence of supposedly strong and visionary leadership.

Yet it seems to be quite widely believed that having people called 'leaders' is better than having people called 'managers' or 'bosses' if only because it signals an intention to be 'nice' on the part of bosses. Who would not want to work for a servant leader, or a compassionate leader, or an authentic leader – to take some of the popular terms and readymade phrases from the language of leadership? In any event, the evidence we have on the deterioration of corporate life for ordinary staff (to which we turn in a moment), strongly suggests such terms are more likely to be camouflage for bad behaviour than motives for doing good. Even when we might give them the benefit of the doubt and assume bosses actually are genuine in their intent, terms like servanthood, compassion and empathy are usually dead-ends. They are just too seductive and easy to signal, but in reality very, very hard to do, especially in light of the commercial and other pressures bosses are under.

Are Chief Executives Overpaid?

For instance, in the UK, between 2009 and 2014, while the economy grew by 10%, real wages fell by 6%; similarly in the US, the incomes of 95% of households were lower in 2016 than they had been in 2007 (Edgar, 2018). In other words, most people are getting paid *less* in real terms than ten years ago – in spite of overall economic growth – and in spite of the claim to servanthood or compassionate leadership made by a significant number of bosses. Indeed, a further puzzle about leadership's current popularity lies on the other side of the pay equation: the huge growth in the salaries of people like CEOs (including the salaries of many of the people who like to think of themselves as 'servant leaders'). As Deborah Hargreaves has shown in her recent book *Are Chief Executives Overpaid?*:

> In the US in 1965, the ratio [of top pay to average pay] was – on average – 20 to 1, but from that period, chief executive pay rose by almost 1,000 per cent while workforce wages went up only 11 per cent and the ratio today is 347 to 1. The UK has been on a similar trajectory with the average ratio for the FTSE 100 now at 129 to 1 (Hargreaves, 2019: 110).

Similarly, writing about the situation in the UK (though the conditions he speaks of are closely mirrored in most countries of the Global North), Rory Scothorne (2018: 40–1) shows that:

> In 2004–5, official statistics suggested that 12 million people [out of a total population of some 60 million] lived in poverty. In 2014–15, the figure was 13.5 million, roughly the same proportion of a growing population. Yet during that time, the number of families who live in poverty but have one or more adults in work rose from 2 million to 7.4 million. The … increasingly precarious nature of life above the poverty line means these figures probably downplay the true extent of poverty, since people may dip below the threshold multiple times during the year. 'Hard work' the rhetorical wedge dividing the working class into 'strivers' and feckless 'scroungers' is now visibly detached from the promise of disposable income or job security.

If we accept that leadership is, at least in part, about having followers, then since the turn of the century, increasing numbers of low-skilled jobs, poor pay and precarious employment for many must surely have made workers even less likely to be the 'followers' of their bosses in any meaningful sense? Indeed, as Scothorne goes on to say, because they are typically employed more and more by agencies or work on a self-employed basis, when many people do go to work, 'they experience novel forms of exploitation that make it impossible to identify their boss, never mind hate them' (2018: 41).

The pro-boss stance implied by using 'leadership' might be more evident if we contrast it with some of the other terms for corporate bosses. Even if we stick to terms used in more formal writing, and leave aside labels widely used by journalists criticizing CEOs – such as fat cat – how about the term used in the title of a 1956 book by the sociologist C. Wright Mills: *The Power Elite*? Or more recently, the title of a 2014 book by the journalist Owen Jones: *The Establishment*? Either term – 'power elite' or 'the establishment' – juxtaposed against 'business leader' starts to suggest the inherent partiality and pro-boss nature of the term 'leader'. Indeed, we believe it is a symptom of how unquestioned market capitalism is becoming in our society that the mundane use of 'leader' as a synonym for 'boss' is becoming not just popular and widely accepted – but virtually unnoticed.

In the light of these arguments, we thought it appropriate to end this chapter with the words of the former politician and activist, the late Tony Benn. He recommended (see Nichols, 2014) that anyone in positions of economic, social and political power should always be asked the following five questions:

1. What power have you got?
2. Where did you get it from?
3. In whose interests do you use it?
4. To whom are you accountable?
5. How do we get rid of you?

These are the sorts of questions that people like CEOs and others at the top of organizational life should regularly be asked. The language of leadership, however, significantly reduces the chances of such challenges ever being made.

5
BUILDING SANTA'S WORKSHOP

Let us start by saying, as a way of summarizing what we have covered so far in the book, a bit more about what we think leadership is *not*. For us and for several reasons, leadership is not management. Now, usually when this sentiment is expressed – as we have already seen – people tend to mean something like: leadership is more than management; or that leadership means being a really good or special kind of manager; or if you are only being a manager then that is not good enough, you need to be a leader as well. We do not mean this sort of thing at all. We mean, much more simply, that doing management or being in a management role is not really anything like 'leadership' (as it has been understood historically) at all.

In common with most people who have spent a few years working in different kinds of organizations, we have each been lucky to have had some very good managers. These are the kinds of manager who – when you mention their name to colleagues – make people smile and encourage them to swap good stories: they are 'one of the good ones' who got the position on merit (or at least, did not get there for entirely the wrong reasons). In contrast, and again this will be true for most people with a few years on their career clock, we have also had to suffer one or two horrible managers. These are the kinds of people whose names make people roll their eyes, or even provoke silence and sadness – they are more deserving of help and pity than any position of responsibility: the bullies and wrong 'uns who perhaps only got their position because of who they know.

We would never have called *any* of our managers 'leaders' though. Indeed it would make us uncomfortable even to think of them as 'leaders' – whether they were exceptionally good or exceptionally bad, or somewhere in between. This is because neither of us feel the need or desire to be so under someone else's influence. We want to think for ourselves, not be swayed by admiration for someone we think of as being our 'leader'. Even so, as we have already pointed out a number of times, routinely now, people in (what we would think of as) management positions, in different sectors, are described as being in 'leadership roles'.

Let's Get Cynical

It is easy to be cynical about this, and we welcome cynicism. We want to encourage and celebrate a kind of active, purposeful cynicism. Indeed, we want to spread cynicism because it seems that the language of leadership is often embraced without people stopping to think. It is stocked with the readymade phrases Orwell advises us to be constantly on guard against. From our own experience, and from the experience of friends and relatives, people are cynical about this language in many workplaces already, and certainly not just in universities. Of course, just as football punditry is often nonsense (as we saw in Chapter 2), there is a great deal about modern day work and modern day management that makes people cynical. It is not difficult to ridicule a way of talking about the world where we 'reach out' or 'touch base' to 'facilitate' and 'share' 'best practice' 'winning' 'buy-in' to 'leverage' 'value' 'going forward', 'pushing the envelope' to be 'best in class' and 'paradigm shift'. Plenty of people have written about the corrosive effects of this kind of euphemistic froth, although leadership seems to have had a comparatively easy ride so far. It seems overdue for serious criticism because many people in business schools and in other workplaces take this language seriously.

That in itself would suggest it is worthy of studying and understanding, but there is another reason too. As cynics, we freely acknowledge that a lot of people would say that they are interested in and passionate about leadership. We are just as interested in 'leadership' as many of those working in the leadership industry, but our take on leadership is radically different. We are also just as passionate about 'leadership' – in the sense that we hate it. We hate phrases like: 'showed leadership', 'real leadership', 'effective leadership', 'team leader', 'thought leadership', 'authentic leadership', 'servant leadership' and so on. Indeed we hate this language so much we sometimes refer to it as 'leader-shit': a subspecies of bullshit. But what is going on exactly? If leadership is a completely empty or meaningless term in this setting then why is the leader-shit being sprayed around like an aerosol, or like manure from a muck spreader?

Leaders, as we understand them, are people who attract and command large numbers of followers, and in this respect they are somehow distinctive and – for want of a better term – 'special' in some way. There is, as Keith Grint (2011) has written, something 'sacred' about leadership. But this language has become so widespread that it is used in mundane settings to put a kind of gloss on relationships in the workplace. This language tries to make these relationships super-ordinary in some senses, and in doing that it tries to deny that work is itself 'work' as such. People do not *work* for leaders, they *follow* them. This is the full force of leader-shit. It disguises the unavoidable fact that relations at work are almost always based on relationships of exchange.

The Pro-Elite, Cultural Associations of 'Leadership'

Despite the best efforts and intentions of even the most thoughtful, critical thinkers who write about leadership today, the language of leadership is irredeemably flawed. Rather than try to rescue it, we think that it would be more effective to be challenging others who use it, and stop using the language of leadership ourselves. One reason for doing so is that 'leader' brings with it overwhelmingly pro-elite cultural associations. But what do we mean by pro-elite cultural associations? We mean a set of assumptions that build up a picture of the social world that supports the interests of those in power. We are against leadership because we believe that any description of a social setting that uses the term 'leader' automatically also writes certain other assumptions into that setting. These include:

- That there is only one legitimate source of power and authority – the leader.
- That other actors in that setting are necessarily subordinate to that so-called leader.
- The nature of this subordination goes beyond what would be a simple reporting relationship (of the kind that one would have to a manager) because there is something 'special' about leaders. It is a follower relationship.
- Finally, it writes in the assumption that people in that setting share the same goals, because this is the nature of followers.

We can contrast each of these assumptions with what is implied in use of the term 'manager'.

The Value of 'Management'

'Manager' can be a very valuable and useful way to describe an employment relationship. If we have a 'manager' (as opposed to a 'leader'), we can accept much more readily that they are not necessarily the only legitimate source of power and authority. They should represent the interests of the owners of the organization (who in many cases are the shareholders) and they could represent a general point of view that is 'management'. However, the use of the term 'manager' implies that there are other legitimate, divergent interests – such as those of the workers. The workers' interests could be represented by another source of power, such as trade unions, for example.

Also, whilst workers are indeed subordinate to managers in terms of whom they report to, there is nothing mystical or special implied in this relationship. No shared vision or charisma or razzmatazz is needed, thank you very much. In this model of work organizations and the employment relationship, subordinates do not even need to agree with their managers – or like them – they just need to do their job to some specified standards. In contrast, the image of an employment relationship where there is a leader suggests that there is some kind of special influence at work, since they have and inspire 'followers'. As the assumptions above suggest, these followers must also agree with the goals that their leader has – or else why would they follow them?

A Santa's Workshop

These pro-elite cultural associations mean that whenever we talk about an organization's 'leaders' (however casually we may use the term – and even if we are criticizing these 'leaders') then we are joining in a grand, collective lie. The lie comes about because 'leadership' involves a remaking of workplaces. It involves turning them from sites of contest, inequality and a plurality of interests into – at least in the imagination of the speaker – a kind of Santa's workshop, where everyone is a happy elf, united behind a celebration and glorification of the people in charge.

At this point it is interesting to look at another quote from *Animal Farm*, where Squealer (the pig who acted as Napoleon's henchman) explained the 'new arrangements' to the rest of the animals:

> Do not imagine, comrades, that leadership is a pleasure! On the contrary, it is a deep and heavy responsibility. No one believes more firmly than Comrade Napoleon that all animals are equal. He would be only too happy to let you make your decisions for yourselves. But sometimes you might make the wrong decisions, comrades, and then where should we be? (Orwell, 1945/2000: 40).

Orwell's Napoleon deceived other animals by pretending to be their equal, and by pretending to have their best interests at heart. He played on the idea of leadership as a burden. The contemporary uses of 'leadership' in organizations involve similar deception. They also involve the fiction of a common purpose, and in addition we have a mythical figure of the leader. In using the language of leadership, we are not just celebrating this heroic figure, we are also conspiring in the denigration of others, or at least in re-sculpting workers so they fit the profile of someone who shares the interests of the organization. Diverging interests and tensions (for instance between workers' wages and company profits) get airbrushed away because workers are 'led' and their 'leader' shares their goals. To explain this it is worth looking at the basics of the employment relationship.

A Sketch of the Employment Relationship

In our view, the employment relationship essentially involves striking a bargain between groups with different interests. On the one hand, workers sell their skills, time and efforts for a price (let's call this 'labour'). On the other hand, owners and managers who are supposed to be the representatives or stewards of owners try to realize the most value that they can from workers' skills, time and efforts (let's call this 'capital'). Because it is in labour's interests to be paid as much as possible, and it is in capital's interests to extract as much value as possible from that relationship, the interests of these groups differ and are often in tension. Put simply, if you keep putting up wages, you have to cut profits (all other things being equal).

This is not to suggest that owners and managers cannot be colleagues and friends with those whom they manage; or that owners and managers are necessarily callous or uncaring; or that workers are always and inevitably massively exploited. It is not to suggest that owners and managers are right or wrong, or that they should have more or less power than they do. Neither does this simple sketch rule out different kinds of incentives and ownership models which could bring the interests of labour and capital closer together. It does not mean that successful enterprises cannot be mutually beneficial to labour and capital, nor does it claim to cover all different kinds of organization (partnerships, family businesses, public sector organizations, charities, mutuals, etc.). Equally it does not rule out different models of profit and risk sharing.

What this simple sketch *does* suggest though is that built into the employment relationship there is a continuing struggle about what is fair (along with who is in control). There are many, many different kinds of organization, but if you sign up at some level to this simple sketch then you can see how conflict is almost hardwired into this relationship. Another way to express this is to say that there is what has been called 'structured antagonism' in this relationship – things that are fixed and immovable and that are sources of continual tension and struggle (even if they do not result in open conflict).

The Useful Fiction of a Common Cause

Our point is that calling owners and managers (and also other kinds of elites) 'leaders' can be seen as an attempt to draw a veil over this antagonism. The employment relationship then becomes seen as no longer primarily about exchange, or as striking a bargain between wages and profits. Instead, there is the pretence of a common cause. We have already seen this pretence break down in the last chapter when we contrasted the 'leadership' section on the website at TGI Fridays (where everything seems happy and cooperative) with the letter an employee sent to the CEO alleging that the CEO grossly mistreats her workforce.

Here we can usefully come back to our fundamental point, that the language of leadership is not just being used merely to *describe* relations at work, but to *reshape* them. The sense in which we are anti-leadership is that we are very cynical and critical about what the very word 'leadership' does to social relations. Our arguments here have resonance when we compare them to the quote from *Animal Farm* that we used above. It suits the interests of those who have the most power and who reap the most rewards if they can convince all other employees that they have interests in common and are doing the best they can for everyone:

that 'all animals are equal'. Napoleon tries to justify his own position of comfort and superiority by an appeal to inequality and complaints about the 'heavy responsibility' of leadership. This idea of common enterprise is generally a fiction, and because this fiction often does not stand up to any scrutiny it needs to be sustained and continually refreshed. The language of leadership is very useful in perpetuating this fiction because 'leader' implies that others in the organization (implicitly, but rarely actually called followers) have the same goal and the same values.

Diagnosing, Classifying and Commodifying 'Leadership'

As we have said earlier in this chapter, we have no issue accepting that there is such a thing as leadership. Leadership as a process is most likely an inevitable part of human societies. A lot of work has been written about the process of leadership – often this work discusses what can be taken as examples of good leadership and what can be copied. Then there are some closely related questions about leaders. Some writers and academics identify the kinds of people who are model leaders, or they specify desirable characteristics in leaders. Many more people have turned leadership into a commodity – they claim they are able to help people become leaders and then charge them for the privilege. However, we are not particularly interested in these kinds of questions, which as we suggested in Chapter 2 are more the province of the leadership industry. The question we are interested in comes before these questions of diagnosis, classification and commodification. We are interested in the language of leadership itself and what happens to social relations when this is used. When we say that we are 'against leadership' we are against the effects and use of this language.

If we celebrate 'leaders' and 'leadership' in organizations, what happens is we start to shape everyone 'below' this leader into a 'follower'; each of whom is dependent on their leader for their work identity. This is building a Santa's workshop in terms of a celebration and glorification of the people in charge and in terms of a series of pro-elite cultural associations. Another way of saying this would be that the language of leadership – in the context of organizational life – is pro-hegemonic (a hegemon being a system of rule). Uses of 'leadership' reproduce a system of rule that underpins contemporary relations of exchange, and that also is set up to support the intensification of work. When we bring a 'leader' into the workplace that implies common purpose and it also implies that they can get more from workers – as 'followers' – than they would otherwise give.

If we routinely talk of organizations as having leaders, or as the workers being led, then we imply a form of rule that is based on shared purpose. Yet in many – indeed surely most – for-profit organizations (as well as most of the public sector) we would say that common purpose is simply not the reality. Companies are profitable *precisely because* they recognize how to create a gap between the interests (and costs) of their workforce, such as pay, pension, rights and the value realized in the marketplace by their workers' efforts. As we showed in Chapter 4, company 'leaders' are often rewarded on the basis of being able to open up this gap – to create greater savings, efficiencies and productivity. The celebration and glorification of a leader draws a veil over this gap – it is a useful fiction that disguises this structured antagonism.

We all know from our own work experiences that our interests, and the interests of our organizations, can diverge. This is true for anyone who has ever 'had to work late', or who has wanted to take the day off but instead gone into work, or has 'not had time for lunch', or who has celebrated 'Saint Monday' (i.e. the practice of illicitly skipping work on a Monday), or been in any of a thousand such situations. Indeed, being paid or 'compensated' for the work we do is an explicit acknowledgement of this divergence of interests.

Returning to our structured antagonism between profits and wages, one could argue that the interests of workers and those who own businesses will always diverge. This is because no-one working for a company (who is working to the required standard) is paid what they are 'worth'. They might be being paid a comparable or better wage than other people in other settings, but if you paid people the exact same sum as their labour was worth, then a firm would not realise any profits.

Even so, rather than acknowledge these kinds of tensions and differences, many modern workplaces are continually being redescribed and reinvented as common enterprises with shared interests. Employees are 'colleagues', 'associates' or 'partners' and organizations are often euphemistically called 'teams' or 'families', who set out and then periodically revisit and renew common goals, mission, values, purpose, a shared vision and so on. The modern workplace is a world where using 'we' takes on a special resonance. It supports the use of commands and directions, at the same time as maintaining the continual fiction that throughout the organization there is a common purpose and a common set of goals.

Unmasking Corporate Power

An important effect that the language of leadership has/does, therefore, is to disguise relations of power. Simply using 'leader' is pro-hegemonic because it provides us with useful fictions – that followers are not coerced in any way but that they are willing, that there is shared purpose – that leaders are somehow special and can rightfully claim some supremacy and so on. We have discussed this in terms of the employment relationship, and the tension between labour and capital, but another aspect to this is corporate power. To introduce how academics who write about organizations think about relations of power it can be helpful to draw a distinction between two kinds or modes of power.

First, and this is the most conventional and typical view of power, often in organizations we see power exercised in specific and very visible ways. Particular actions and incidents can underline who is 'in charge'. Sometimes, people who are 'in charge' can make it clear that work has to be done in a certain way or by a certain time. Some people in organizations give orders or demand answers or are clearly the decision-makers, some set and communicate deadlines, others approve or deny requests, some people get to decide whether or not something can be reimbursed or is legitimate expenditure, some decide whether or not a form is correctly filled in and so on. This kind of 'official' power is one that we can readily 'place'. It is either in a certain setting (a function or office/department or procedure) or it is, in a way, a kind of power that can be carried around – so it is seen most easily in the decisions and actions of people who 'have' power. Sometimes this kind of power is called 'episodic' – because it is a kind of power that is seen in specific people or places and exercised at particular times. For example we can imagine questions like: 'Why are you late?' 'Shouldn't you be over there?' 'Have you replied to that customer yet?' These are expressions of episodic power. In terms of the structured antagonism in the employment relationship the times when one is paid, or pay is frozen or raised are expressions of episodic power. The kinds of moments that exemplify this form of episodic power are often going to be what first comes to mind when we think of 'corporate power'.

Everyday Power

Second though, there is another hidden dimension to power. This is because what we do in our work lives is shaped or even controlled by things that could ordinarily go unnoticed and are just part of daily organizational life. This mundane, or ordinarily unseen kind of power, is not as readily visible or identifiable and so it is something that we have to trace more carefully – by looking in depth at the details of everyday social relations and by studying things that might seem trivial or mundane. This includes the use of language, practices and conventions, and what is loosely called culture – a whole set of basic assumptions about 'the way we do things around here'. To make for a contrast with episodic power, we will give this second kind of power another name – 'everyday power'. Many people writing from a critical perspective on management share an interest in this second expression or mode of power.

This distinction between episodic and everyday power becomes helpful and relevant because it helps us to connect 'corporate power' to the 'language of leadership'. The terms and phrases in the language of leadership, as shown back in Table 1.1 in the introduction, can be most clearly associated with this first expression or mode of episodic power (showing leadership, being a certain kind of leader, being in a role and so on). These show where power is. However, it is the *effects* of using these terms that we are interested in, and these are associated with what we call everyday power.

As an example, the following question is about everyday power: 'What does it mean if we now call managers "leaders", how does it change relations at work?' The attention to language is important because it gives us insights into the different ways in which power is sustained and used, and made legitimate in the course of everyday work practices. As the sub-title of our book suggests, we believe that when we are discussing the language of leadership we are not talking simply about language as such – we are also talking about corporate power. Using the phrase 'the language of leadership' is our way of trying to draw rich connections between language and power. Whenever terms like 'leadership' or 'leader', 'followership' or 'follower' are used these words are 'doing' things. There is a kind of deep architecture at work here because these are foundational terms that build up a certain picture of social relations.

In reality, many workplaces are sites of contest, where there are multiple goals and values and often these differ according to where in the hierarchy we find ourselves. There are typically large differences in terms of pay, power, autonomy, security, employability, the scope of work and so on. Frontline workers are not necessarily the most disadvantaged since they might enjoy a continuity and regularity to their work which middle managers (who have to cope with doubts from below and demands from above) may envy. None of this is to deny that the workplace is an important source of solidarity, meaning, identity and often enjoyment. Of course there can be many stresses that come with positions of greater responsibility too.

We want to unearth these foundations and make visible the work that the language of leadership does in perpetuating fiction. We want to do this, in part, so that we – and anyone who shares similar discomfort – can at least make a start in unravelling this fiction. We want to argue as strongly as possible that, even if they are contrary to the vast leadership industry and even if our views are controversial, that our basic argument rests on things that are plain and evident for all to see. What we want to show is that we have sound reasons for our cynicism which are both intellectual and political.

The significance of the shift in rhetoric from management to leadership is profound. This is because of the implications for everyday power. One of the important consequences of the rise in the language of leadership means that the people who used to think of themselves as mere 'managers' can now imagine themselves using a term that makes them sound much grander: they can imagine themselves as 'leaders'.

We would argue that a key reason that the language of leadership has become popular is because it has suited the interests of those who represent corporate power – the bosses or, 'capital'. This language is a pro-elite resource. This resource is a kind of filter through which elites can imagine and project their identities in much more positive (and functionally useful) ways than was the case with the language of management.

Leadership and the Rise of Neo-liberalism

We have shown that definitions of leadership are often completely at odds with what happens in the real world of work. This is because those who take some care to define leadership (at least at the beginning of their books and articles) often go to pains to explain how leadership is special and different from management. But, as is plain to see, in the workplace and in wider society people have simply swapped in the term 'leader' whereas before they used manager. Though we are critical of and reject this language we are at least consistent with the real world – because our basic idea that calling things 'leadership' matters is clearly in line with practice. A few years ago, people started going to the trouble of changing things like, say, the name of the 'senior management team' to the 'senior leadership team' and referring to their CEOs and senior executives as 'leaders'. Meanwhile, consultants started offering 'leadership development' courses and a host of other things changed in how we talk about those in senior positions. People at corporate HQs clearly believe that calling things leadership matters. Indeed, many senior people are increasingly insistent that their job is one of leadership – *not* management; or not merely that of being a head teacher, a nurse, and so on.

One of the things distinguishing our position from this pro-elite position, is that we are not especially concerned with whether someone 'really' is a leader (whatever that might mean). We aren't interested in the five things that make someone a leader rather than a manager or whatever. Our focus is on what the word leadership 'does' and it is intended as *critique*. We think that 'leadership' does many things within organizational life, and within wider society, which urgently need challenging – this is precisely because leadership is now widely celebrated as a cure for all organizational ills.

The current celebration of leadership may be something of a puzzle – in the sense that it seems so far from many people's experience of and views about working life. That is why we think that the change to 'leadership' is not about making the practicalities of life better for everyone. Instead, it can be understood as intimately tied up with a parallel rise in certain ideological preferences. These are spreading throughout Western society and beyond. To us it seems likely that the rise in the celebration of leadership is intimately associated with the march of an ideology that has come to be known as *neo-liberalism*: that is, the naturalization, indeed, the glorification of 'individual self-interest, economic efficiency and unbridled competition' (Steger and Roy, 2010: x).

It is worth reflecting again upon the fact that the last thirty years or so – the period in which leader has become a popular name for the people in charge – has also been the period in which trade union power has all but been destroyed, and ordinary workers have increasingly found themselves on minimum wages, zero-hour contracts and needing to work increasingly excessive hours. Not only this, it has also been a period in which our so-called leaders have enjoyed unprecedentedly and disproportionately higher salaries and bonuses that increase year-on-year – often grossly so. In this kind of context, the language of leadership, even when it is well-intended, does things that can easily be read as naïve – perhaps as something like romantic wish-fulfilment. However, much of the language of leadership can do things that are actively negative from the point of view of ordinary workers; not least, it can provide forms of camouflage for self-serving corporate interests.

We are not suggesting that there has been a conspiracy somehow to inject the language of leadership into corporate life. We do not imagine anything like Bush and Blair plotting together (between prayer sessions no doubt) on how they could please their corporate friends and dupe workers into compliance. Apart from anything else, the drift towards leadership over the last thirty years has been too informal, too evolutionary for such possibilities. A more likely explanation is that the emerging neo-liberal consensus (or perhaps the consensus is now taken for granted – see Bridgman et al, 2018) is giving ideas about organizational leadership, which have been around in academia for many years, new traction in the popular imagination.

Mark started his career in health care back in the early 1980s. In those days, when unions were much more powerful, the idea of calling senior managers 'leaders' would seem ridiculous – to the managers as much as to the workers. This is because the political situation at that time was such that the gap and the structured antagonism between managers and workers that we drew attention to earlier in the chapter was much more evident to everyone involved.

In other words, it seems a strong possibility that the fact 'leader' has become acceptable as an apparent synonym for boss is largely down to the increased *everyday power* of bosses. The use of 'leader' and 'follower' is as useful to those at the top of big business – and as congruent with their interests – as other forms of neo-liberal rhetoric. These include the redefinition of job insecurity as 'free agency' or the 'gig economy', the celebration of 'flexibility' (which means flexibility that suits organizational interests), or the portrayal of billionaire tycoons as 'regular guys'. When workers can be controlled through their freedoms the defenders of capitalism no longer have to crush labour resistance. Redefining themselves – the defenders of capitalism – as leaders (with workers now cast as followers) is appealing as one potential avenue towards everyday control. This is because it tends to hollow out classical notions of organizational politics. The language of leader and follower erases any debate about alienation or exploitation and remakes 'conflict' into an exercise of 'problem-solving' and 'team-building'.

It might be useful, therefore, to think of the language of leadership as a kind of second-generation mutation of the language of management. In the current neo-liberal environment, the leadership mutation is turning out to be more successful (i.e. more persuasive and attractive) than the management original. It is even, if we wanted to be really pessimistic, starting to threaten the very survival of the language of management.

Summary of Part I

Around the late 1970s, something momentous started to happen across the West. Ever since, we have witnessed the seemingly ineluctable triumph of the people who run business over rivals such as the unions and the regulatory state. Their triumph has endured, even after a financial meltdown in the first decade of the twenty-first century; even today it continues to affect all our lives profoundly.

Since the early 1980s, many of the economic policies pursued in the West have probably made most of us poorer than we otherwise would have been. 'Austerity' and the precarious forms of work many are left with today, are merely the latest manifestations of these policies. The organization of public services has also changed radically – having become saturated in the logic of the market. However, in spite of being run by people who are now called 'leaders', many public services are failing the needs of ordinary people. At the same time as making most people poorer, the very same policies have made the people at the apex of the business world (those who are now so often known as 'leaders') extraordinarily richer than they otherwise would have been.

It is in these wider contexts that we are against 'leadership'. We have argued throughout this section of the book that the recent popularization of the term 'leader' as a synonym for people we used to refer to as bosses or managers is both a symptom of the triumph of business interests and a factor that makes contesting the changes even harder.

The point about the language of 'leadership' is that, in parallel with relatively easily measurable economic changes, there have also been rather more subtle changes. One of these has been a gradual drift in the language we use to talk about work and our working lives. Unsurprisingly, this drift in language has gone in the same direction as the economic policies; it too has reinforced the advantages enjoyed by the people in charge. No-one has been consciously orchestrating these changes, though. What seems to have happened is that the sorts of words which make the work of top people sound glamorous and appealing have, over time, gradually become increasingly favoured by people who can influence opinion: politicians, the media, celebrities; even certain academics have played a role in the process. In turn, these glamorous-sounding terms have found a fertile cultural soil in which to take root and grow. What this has meant is that by today many of us now tend to use these positive terms routinely, barely reflecting upon them or even noticing the nature of the language we use.

PART II
'Leadership' as Rhetoric

6
LABELS MATTER

To be able to talk about anything, even in the most mundane situations, we are necessarily forced into choosing particular words from a range of available options. For example, if either of us ever go to a social event with our 'other halves' (the reason we've used this odd term becomes clear in a moment), we both sometimes find ourselves wondering whether to introduce them to other people as 'my partner' or as 'my wife'. Both terms are accurate and legitimate descriptions to use, but 'partner' and 'wife' are clearly not synonyms. Indeed, one of the reasons we might pause before making this particular choice is that the two alternatives can have different cultural, social and political connotations. Each of these labels refers to a social fact, and both are widely in use, but both have the capacity to do different things beyond merely describing the relationship.

The choice of 'partner' over 'wife' might communicate something about our values and beliefs in respect of personal relationships: that we feel different kinds of relationship (such as civil partnerships, for example) are of equivalent worth, or that we would not want to claim implicitly that we enjoyed some kind of superiority or entitlement because of state sanctions or tradition. Even the fact it is us (as men) doing the introducing can carry connotations of patriarchy.

One of the more progressive things about contemporary life – not least because of the influence of feminism – is most of us are more conscious that the words we choose can, and often do matter: in and of themselves. The idea that words matter in this way was not so widely believed a generation or two ago. As is well known, there are a range of terms that used to go more or less unnoticed – or that were assumed to be innocent or unimportant – that are now likely to be censured in mainstream society. This is because they are widely believed to 'do things', in themselves, like expressing forms of sexism for example. Analogously, and like all words do, the terms 'leader' and 'leadership' have effects – whatever our intention may be when we use them.

Language Works Us

All of us rely on default terms which we rarely reflect on much. These ready-made phrases tend to appear to us simply as natural and obvious, coming, as it were, pre-scripted, often by our cultural and social backgrounds. They also do things beyond setting out a state of affairs about an aspect of the world. Indeed, they can have a particular capacity to shape our attitudes and thinking. The danger of such readymade terms is precisely that we do not think about them. This is because they provide us with specific lenses through which to view the world. However, because they are unexamined, they tend to give us the illusion that no lens is involved – that the terms describe the world as it really is.

For instance, for some people, always referring to couples who have undergone wedding ceremonies as 'married' might seem a natural and obvious thing to do; simply the statement of a legal fact that is not worth wasting time reflecting upon. Of course, we clearly are stating a legal fact when we choose to call a couple who have undergone a wedding ceremony 'married'. However, especially if we invariably use this term when talking about relationships of this kind – as an unexamined default – then the label also does things beyond merely stating a fact. Perhaps, for example, in invariably talking about being married we tacitly give marriage a higher status and recognition at the expense of others types of relationships – whether or not we intend to do so. Indeed, in using the term 'marriage' in this way we are likely to be read as betraying something about our own beliefs: maybe, for instance, that we think marriage *should* enjoy a higher status than other forms of relationship (again, regardless of what we feel we might actually believe).

The choice of words we use when say, writing this book, or a company report, may well feel more self-consciously deliberate, especially compared with day-to-day conversations. Still, even in this sort of context, the language we choose 'does things' over and above merely setting out a state of affairs. It does things, furthermore, however carefully we make our word choices, and whether we like it or not. Indeed, something that training in a particular academic discipline does (or that socialization into a particular corporate environment does) is it provides us with a specialist language of terms with which to work. However, this language also 'works' us because the limits of our language are the limits of our ideas and our imaginations. 'Language is never innocent' James Berlin argued (1996: 131); and as Roger Fowler (1991: 10) suggested in the same vein: 'anything that is said or written about the world is articulated from a particular ideological position: language is not a clear window, but a refracting, structuring medium.'

With such claims in mind, what we are suggesting is that the term 'leadership' itself – and its corollary, 'follower' – have become for many simply default terms. Leadership is a term many of us might use routinely for talking about any kind of power or authority in organizations *without thinking about it much*, and therefore leadership becomes a term that appears merely to set out a state of affairs as facts. What we show in this chapter, however, is that using the language of leadership refracts rather than reflects (what we might take to be) reality. It does things to and with reality rather than merely representing what reality supposedly 'is'.

'Leadership' as Science?

We can sometimes think of the social sciences, and subjects like management studies as trailing behind other disciplines in the 'natural' or 'hard' sciences – like physics and chemistry. In these natural sciences, people are more comfortable using terms like 'fact' or 'truth' when drawing on established insights. They are able to 'prove' things. Many of the insights from physics and chemistry have been the basis for things that we take for granted and that are embedded in daily life. Telling the time, using transportation and a million other features of life go unquestioned. These things are only taken for granted and embedded in daily life and unquestioned because they happen with unwavering regularity. They are based on what we would tend to call, at least since Isaac Newton, scientific 'laws'.

Once we are working with theories that have been tested, and whose outcomes happen with regularity we are on much firmer ground when we are trying to make predictions. This feels like the domain of 'proper' science. In subjects like art, history or literature, by way of contrast, there are very few laws, and everything seems to be subject to interpretation; though there may well still be conventions and schools, or powerful figures influencing how things are understood. Management studies and other social sciences seem to be in between these two ends of an apparent art-science spectrum. Indeed, there is a well-worn question about management: 'Is management an art or a science?' Unsurprisingly, this has also become a well-worn question about leadership, though many leadership academics insist that what they do is science.

One way to think about these differences is in terms of a hierarchy of the sciences – or academic disciplines, as shown in Table 6.1.

TABLE 6.1 A Simple Hierarchy of the Sciences

Mathematics
V
Astronomy
V
Physics
V
Chemistry
V
Biology
V
Sociology
V
The Humanities

As we move down the list in Table 6.1, we are moving further away from terms like proof, fact and law and towards greyer areas of increasing uncertainty and unpredictability. Instinctively perhaps, you could see our claim that the language of leadership is a pro-elite resource as being much lower down this hierarchy. The disciplines at the top of this hierarchy are taken to command greater respect because they deal in certainties – in terms of the things they study and in terms of the predictions they make (although at the very frontiers of knowledge there is always uncertainty in any discipline). Physicists, say, also have much greater consensus among themselves in terms of the definitions they use for the things they study, and in terms of preceding theories and findings – their 'building blocks'. They have more or less agreed definitions of, and ways to measure, force, mass, pressure, energy, motion and so on.

In management (or leadership) studies by contrast, we do not have this kind of consensus. We can quote what some people have said, or we might speak about a more or less successful school or tradition. However, academics working in organization studies do not even agree, for example, on what an 'organization' is. People in the same department, working side by side in the same field of organization studies – who even write with one another – could disagree on this.

They might ask each other a series of questions, and agree or disagree on the answers to them; questions such as: is an organization essentially a political coalition, or is it more like a brain, or is it a machine, or is it more like an organism; or is the term 'organization' a convenient myth that we use to describe ways in which individual people are connected; does it really make sense to say an organization 'does' things, or even what an organization 'thinks' or 'learns', or is it people who 'do' things (and think, and learn)? This lack of consensus among supposed experts might seem strange, but then if you ask two people working in the same organization – or even the same 'team' – how they would define their own work or their organization or team you would be likely to reveal similar differences.

These differences in terms of definitions are not just theoretical questions that we can simply ignore when focusing on practice. This is because they affect people's lived experiences at work and the labels we give to things affect the social world. For example, a question like: 'is it only people who choose, or can we meaningfully say that organizations choose?' becomes really important if we are trying to say who, or what, is responsible for pollution, malpractice and so on.

Perhaps even more fundamentally, we do not even have a universally accepted definition of 'work'. Taking this further, leaving aside 'leaders' for a moment, we do not really agree what it is that even managers do, and we do not agree on what it is that you have to do in order to be a manager. There is no consensus definitively as to whether any particular action counts as 'management'. Once we get into particular aspects of management the picture becomes even more confused. There is no consensus in relation to how to define and measure 'performance' for example, and similarly there is no consensus on how to measure other core terms like 'innovation', or 'learning', or 'satisfaction', or 'commitment', or 'entrepreneurship' and so on.

If, at this point, we were still making comparisons between physics and management studies then any of these terms could be said to be as important to an organization as mass, energy or motion are to physics. But the lack of consensus in management means that there are many different ways of seeing all of these things. This is because the social world is rather more ambiguous and difficult to pin down categorically than at least the kinds of basic phenomena physicists look at (mass, energy, etc.). Fundamentally, this is because the social world is continually being made and interpreted in terms of values and ideologies and crucially, for our purposes here, *through language*.

The hierarchy we have shown in Table 6.1 is a simplification of course. For instance, there are some disciplines that are difficult to place because they can have more or less formal elements to them. Philosophy could incorporate propositional logic (a highly formal language which can be used to describe mathematics) and it can also deal with questions in terms of aesthetics (the realm of the humanities). This can mean that sub-disciplines or schools within one discipline can diverge radically from the mainstream of their parent discipline. Management studies itself is broad in this way. Indeed, it is often more diverse than some of the longer established academic disciplines because it borrows from them. There are, as mentioned, some branches of management (for instance operational research) which draw on formulae and equations to solve more abstract problems, placing them nearer the top of this simple hierarchy, than the kind of research we ourselves tend to do (which comes pretty close to the humanities).

Closed and Open Systems

As well as thinking about these sorts of issues in terms of a hierarchy, sometimes people talk about these kinds of general differences between disciplines in terms of their relating to closed or open systems. In closed systems we know all the parameters that can influence outcomes. In contrast, open systems are those that are less predictable. This contrast could be described as being like the difference between predicting the path of a snooker ball once it is struck (a closed system) and predicting whether a player is going to take on a particular shot in the first place (an open system).

We need to admit this contrast between the player's mind and the path of a ball is a simplification on two fronts. On the one hand, as anyone who has watched snooker would acknowledge, it can be very difficult – if not impossible – to predict outcomes in even comparatively simple, closed systems. On the other hand, advances in neuroscience might mean we could predict whether a player was about to choose a cautious or risky shot (if we were able to wire them up to the appropriate machinery, or perhaps if we could track their eye movements and pupil dilation). Even so, it is not difficult to make the case that predicting outcomes in systems that involve a 'human element' is usually much harder.

Although that could be a source of pride, or symbol that one was working on something particularly important and meaningful, social scientists often feel like poorer cousins to those working in the natural sciences. In fact social scientists are often described as suffering from 'physics envy'. This term describes a kind of deep-seated, existential anxiety: that we do not have the same ability to explain, predict or control things in the way physicists and others do.

This way of representing a hierarchy of disciplines is well understood and the general sentiment of 'physics envy' will also be familiar to many readers. If we may, we would like to invite you for a moment to try to visualize this: 'a scientist in their working environment'. What comes to mind?

...

... imagine a scientist ...

...

What did you see? The kind of figure that we would tend to think of is a white-coated, laboratory-dweller surrounded by machines and technology. Perhaps there were test tubes, maybe they were wearing glasses. There might have been a board with complex equations written on it. If you agree with any of these motifs then you can empathize with why it is that social scientists have this kind of deep-seated anxiety and experience physics envy.

However, and this is actually much more interesting, social scientists don't just lag behind the insights of physicists. Instead, if we think about the things that make us most human, it is often the case that social scientists are trailing behind the kinds of insights we can gain from the humanities: disciplines like history, literature and also philosophy. The figure we have sketched out of a hierarchy of disciplines could just as easily be turned upside down. Because of this, it is from the humanities that we will draw inspiration in examining the 'language of leadership'.

The Linguistic Turn

Many contemporary writers in the social sciences and in management studies show a fascination with language. This fascination with language can be partly understood as the legacy of some influential contributions in the humanities. In particular, an intellectual movement known as the 'linguistic turn' is of central importance to our focus on the language of leadership. This originated in philosophy but it has revolutionized how people understand the relationship between words and the world.

Whilst some philosophers of language used formal theory, symbols and logic in ways that would place their work near the top of the hierarchy of the sciences in Table 6.1, others who made up the linguistic turn were more interested in trying to understand the properties and effects of language. These philosophers of 'natural language' wanted to look beyond questions that were purely to do with meaning and reference and to look beyond a view of language as something that merely describes the social world. The linguistic turn involved nothing less than a fundamental rethinking of the role of language. It became seen as more than a means of describing the social world or of transmitting meaning. Instead language was seen as a form of social life that created meaning and that shaped the social world according to how it was used and according to its context.

This approach to understanding language became characterized as a focus on 'meaning as use' and it involved recognizing that any expression (speaking, or writing, or naming things and describing them) was not purely about conveying meaning, in the way that a logical equation might be imagined to be. Instead, a linguistic expression is part of a broader process of communication, which is a shared activity that takes place in a certain setting and has effects. For the same reasons, understanding ordinary language is not often a question of determining accuracy or truth. Philosophers of ordinary language took much more account of the context for the use of language, as well as considering more explicitly how language shaped the context. Over time, the legacy of these natural language philosophers was that scholars in different communities became more interested in how language was used as a resource that did not simply describe the world, but could actually bring the social world into being.

There was, then, a divide in the linguistic turn between formal theory and logic, and those philosophers of natural language (whose ideas also influenced historians and literary scholars). The ordinary language school was much more interested in the way that language is (and we are now using more contemporary jargon) 'situated' and 'occasioned'. *Situated* suggests that when we think about uses of language – say the uses of the language of leadership – we do not see these uses as the neutral relaying of an idea (in the way we might understand a mathematical or logical equation to be), or conveying something that is either true or false. Rather we see it as something where the meaning of that idea takes shape according to a set of conventions and the practices and understandings of a community. *Occasioned* signals that expressions and uses of language are dependent partly on what has gone before – on traditions, a frame of reference, established meanings, context, culture and so on. This also implies that uses of language have effects on subsequent events.

The Death of the Author, the Impossibility of History

Comparable insights have been developed in other subjects in the humanities. In literature, for example, we have seen a concern with the reader and the way that texts are received and interpreted (rather than taking the perspective that the author has a kind of 'God's eye view'). Closely linked to a concern with the reader is the idea that a text takes on a life of its own and in important senses no longer belongs to the author once it is a candidate for appreciation by others. To take this book as an example, whatever we (or anyone else) might write about leadership we cannot control how its readers will receive it. The final destination, so to speak, or the reception of a text is not something we look back to the author to understand. Instead a text becomes a work in its own right – open to a multitude of readings and interpretations, all of which give power to the audience. This 'death of the author' (Barthes, 1967) is the recognition that there is no ultimate authority for the meaning and sense of a text – not even its creator.

This idea is similar to the linguistic turn in the sense that it means we do not see a text as simply conveying meaning, but instead we pay more attention to the way in which texts are interpreted and received. The linguistic turn gives more power to talk and texts because they are not simply a question of uncovering the truth or communicating in the way an equation might communicate truth. In a comparable way, the idea of the death of the author is that the text has almost unlimited power because we cannot pin meaning down by (for instance), studying the biography of its author.

In history, one of the major insights of the last century is the idea that there is no possibility of a neutral account of history. We cannot have a purely factual chronicle (like a list of the dates of kings and queens, say) and sensibly call this 'history'. Instead any history is always a *kind of* history, one that follows the conventions and prejudices of its age, a history that is characterized as much by what is left out as what is included. The writer Louis Montrose expresses this idea by saying:

> we can have no access to a full and authentic past, a lived material existence ... textual histories necessarily but always incompletely constitute in their narrative and rhetorical forms the 'history' to which they offer access (in Rivkin and Ryan, 1998: 781).

This is what Montrose calls the inescapable 'textuality of history': no matter how sophisticated, or intricate our descriptions of historical events are, these descriptions are always mediated by language. The way we relate history – including history even in the sense of what happened at work yesterday – is a form of storytelling and involves choices about what to include or exclude, what to prioritize, what to downplay. To describe this, the historian Hayden White (1973) invented the term 'emplotment'. White was concerned with what made history more than a retelling or chronicling of events, and with the problem of the impossibility of reproducing events in all their complexity and detail in texts.

For White, emplotment gives us, 'the "meaning" of a story by identifying the kind of story that has been told' (1973: 9). Emplotment is an act that involves going beyond a mere chronicling or sequencing of events to the telling of a story, 'introducing structure that allows making sense of the events reported in a narrative' (Czarniawska, 2012: 758). To understand this more fully we can connect the linguistic turn with the appreciation of a more ancient idea – rhetoric.

Rhetoric and the 'New Rhetoric'

The central concern that scholars working in the linguistic turn have – that language is not purely about the communication of meaning but that it can be a powerful resource – can be usefully linked to the more ancient study of rhetoric. This is understood by Aristotle as the art and science of persuasion (Morrell, 2012). Rhetoric is not principally about the content of arguments used to persuade people, it is about the way that the content in these arguments is put together. Effective ways of organizing content will appeal not just to reason and logic (*logos*), but also to an audience's feelings (*pathos*). Moreover, the character of the speaker (*ethos*) is also important because a credible speaker will be more effective. Devices such as contrasts and lists, for instance, can make arguments seem more persuasive.

In giving importance to emotions and the character of the speaker, as well as identifying the most effective ways to organise content, Aristotle and others foresaw some of the concerns that ordinary language scholars have – that language (including the language of leadership) is not purely about transmitting meaning. There are a great many rhetorical devices which have proven effective in organising the content of messages and Aristotle is the first to explain how and why these are powerful (lists and contrasts as mentioned, and also emphasis, metaphor, simile and so on). So the main learning point from considering rhetoric is to differentiate between content and how this content is *organized*.

Ancient studies of rhetoric gave us great insight into the importance of the speaker (or *rhetor*) and the way they organized the content of their arguments. However, what tended to be overlooked in these approaches was the role of the audience. In more contemporary studies of rhetoric, the audience is seen not just as a passive recipient of a message, but as an active participant. This main contribution to the ancient study of rhetoric, in what has become known as the 'new rhetoric', is similar in some ways to the idea of the death of the author. The rhetor is not simply transmitting meaning or imposing an 'authoritative' interpretation of events, but instead, together with the audience they are collectively engaged in the construction of meaning which is also a function of the context.

Self-fulfilling Prophecies and the Pygmalion Effect

We will draw together these different strands and descendants of the linguistic turn shortly to show how important language is in studying the 'language of leadership'. Before we do so, however, it is also worth identifying two closely related phenomena where our insights come more from social psychology than the humanities: (i) self-fulfilling prophecies and (ii) the Pygmalion effect. Both of these ideas show how, when it comes to describing social phenomena, the labels we use can actually shape those phenomena themselves. If we describe a physical object in terms of its mass, momentum or size these are constants. A snooker ball will always be a certain diameter and weight, but whether we describe these in inches or millimetres, or grams or ounces is irrelevant. In contrast, if we gave a nickname to a player – say Alex 'Hurricane' Higgins or Jimmy 'Whirlwind' White – these sorts of labels might not just be objective descriptions, but rather they could become something they embrace and live up to. If their behaviour did change, inspiring them to take on a riskier style of play, or even more self-destructive lifestyle, the nicknames could be instances of self-fulfilling prophecies and the Pygmalion effect. However (and we promise to say no more about snooker) it is worth expanding on these a little because they are slightly different.

A *self-fulfilling prophecy* meets a number of conditions. It is a kind of prediction which comes true, but which only becomes true because people believe it to be true (otherwise it would be false). A classic example would be a 'run' on a bank. If enough of a bank's customers believe that a bank which is otherwise working well will fail, then they will try to withdraw their money from the bank – which will cause the bank to fail. Another classic example is that of the teacher who labels a pupil bad at maths: the pupil internalizes the teacher's appraisal and so ends up failing their maths exams – regardless of whether they really were 'bad' at maths in the first place. The point is that the initial framing or labelling of a social phenomenon – even if the label is false – is important in influencing the situation and its outcomes.

The 'Pygmalion effect' is named after the play *Pygmalion* by George Bernard Shaw (this play, incidentally, is also the basis of the musical *My Fair Lady*). It is a particular kind of self-fulfilling prophecy. Specifically, the Pygmalion effect is where people have higher than warranted expectations of someone, and these expectations become true because the person lives up to those expectations. If we expect more of someone, our expectations condition our interactions with them, influencing not just their behaviour – but also the way we see their behaviour. In Shaw's play, Henry Higgins is able to transform the flower seller Eliza Doolittle, with some training, into someone who seems to be a princess, because enough people believe her to be one. Famous, real world cases of the Pygmalion effect have been validated using experiments in schools – where teachers are told some randomly chosen students in their class are gifted. Even though the label is randomized, over time the performance of those students said to be gifted improves. Again, the way a situation is described or framed, directly influences the situation. Unlike phenomena in the hard sciences (which we might describe using constants and objective terms), our labels and descriptions of social phenomena directly influence those phenomena.

In other words, and now thinking in terms of 'leadership', merely calling someone a leader is likely to have effects. It may be, to some extent at least, a self-fulfilling prophecy – though not always with happy consequences. The language of leadership has the capacity to transform a mere manager into someone who believes they are (perhaps) somehow charismatic or 'special' or deserving of authority – almost regardless of what they actually do. This could lead to a happy

Pygmalion-type scenario. Alternatively, it could mean we are transforming someone who understands their role (as a manager) primarily in terms of competence into someone who thinks of themselves as somehow 'special' as a leader and now has a greater element of self-delusion in their psyche. This could be someone who in everyday slang has 'drunk the kool aid' or 'believes their own bullshit'. This is an argument we develop in more detail in Chapters 8 and 9. For now, however, we should say that a shorthand way of signalling this fascination with language is to use the term *discourse* ('discourse' can refer to both talk and texts).

Discourse

As we have suggested (drawing together the different strands we have traced back to the linguistic turn) more recent, applied forms of study in the social sciences have focused increasingly on language. 'Discourse' is the broadest idea we want to draw on in thinking about the language of leadership and so we discuss it last in this chapter. When social scientists use the word discourse, they are expressing the idea that language goes beyond merely describing the world, it makes the world (e.g. Fairclough, 1995). The idea of discourse in this sense can be understood as the culmination of these different insights in philosophy, literature, history and rhetoric: the linguistic turn.

The linguistic turn denies the possibility of a 'pure' communication of meaning (because language is always situated and occasioned), and the idea of the death of the author rejects the possibility of one true interpretation of a text (because interpretation is a question for the audience and multiple interpretations are possible). Contemporary historians reject the idea that any account of the past can simply convey 'facts' or 'history' (any history is always a kind of history). Each of these can be understood as different aspects to 'discourse'.

An issue that is important to flag up here is that one of the difficulties of developing insights about discourse is that, even though we are trying to talk about language, we are using the medium of language to do so. Sometimes people describe this kind of dilemma as being 'enmeshed'. Writing about language means we are tangled in a web of existing conventions, practices and understandings. As a result, it is impossible to step outside of this web and view the problems of language or 'discourse' as an independent observer.

The claim to independence is one advantage the philosophers using formal theory could say they had over others interested in ordinary language. They were relying on using symbolic logic to describe language (often this is referred to as using a 'metalanguage' – a language about language). Providing this was a sensible and meaningful thing to do (and ordinary language philosophers doubt this), this could offer a way out of the 'enmeshed' dilemma. A metalanguage could offer an independent place to stand. Table 6.2 below summarizes the ideas in this chapter so far.

TABLE 6.2 The Linguistic Turn and its Descendants

Intellectual Movement	Main Characteristics	Implications for the Language of Leadership
The Linguistic Turn	Across a number of different disciplines, this movement reflects a concern with language as being more than the transmission of meaning but as 'situated' (taking place in a context) and 'occasioned' (shaped by and shaping that context).	Describing something as leadership or calling someone a leader is not a neutral description of a person or situation. It has effects.
Death of the Author	Once a text is 'out there', it can have a multiplicity of meanings depending on the interpretation of multiple audiences. The author is not an authority who can say definitively what the meaning is.	The language of leadership can colonize and infect different spheres of life. Those in the leadership industry appropriate whatever ideas support their own interests. An example is taking Burns' work on political leadership and the idea of 'transformational' leadership and applying it to mundane work settings (discussed in Chapters 8 and 12).
Impossibility of Neutral History	No description of events is purely factual. History is always more than a chronicle of events because it is at some level a story, and events are always emplotted (made into certain kinds of story).	Any description of events at work as being leadership or of someone at work as a leader is fitting them into one particular way of understanding social relations (a world where there are leaders and where leadership happens). Other ways of understanding the world are available.
Rhetoric	Communication through language is not simply about relaying the content of messages, it is also important to consider the way content is organized and to appeal to emotions and the credibility of the speaker.	Messages that are packaged in terms of leadership are trying to recruit a kind of authority that goes beyond the content of these messages. The term leader may (inappropriately) signal credibility and be a way of persuading others to believe what the speaker or writer is claiming.
The 'New Rhetoric'	The audience is not a passive recipient of meaning, they join in the collective making of meaning. This shared activity depends on the context for any communication and on the features of a particular issue or situation. That in turn is a function of pre-existing constraints on communication and depends on things like timing.	Consensus about the language of leadership at work (leadership is 'good', leaders are 'special', organizations need leaders) when there should be different views (it may be inappropriate, leader can be an empty term or it can constrain our understanding of the social world).

Intellectual Movement	Main Characteristics	Implications for the Language of Leadership
Discourse	Words (both talk and texts) do not simply describe the world, they make the world.	Calling things leadership, or someone a leader brings certain kinds of social relations into being.

Challenging the Language of Leadership

In relation to the core theme of this book, these different intellectual traditions help us to challenge the language of leadership. The trouble is, as people who study business and management, there is no independent place to stand. It has become impossible to talk about many issues that are related to (phenomena generally taken to be) leadership in corporations (power, authority, control) without at the same time using some of this language. Across different media there is an incessant chatter about leadership and innumerable books and articles take leadership as their focus.

We cannot hope to fully disentangle or dismantle – or completely unravel this language as independent observers – because we are enmeshed in it ourselves. What we want to do is to draw on all the insights about language we have touched on in this chapter to understand the language of leadership and its effects. This involves considering, as we explain in the next chapter, how leadership is 'performed'.

7
PERFORMING LEADERSHIP

A very common focus in written work on leadership is to try to analyze different activities that are associated with leaders: inspiring people, creating a vision, being a role model, building successful teams and organizations and so on. Sometimes when people describe how leadership is performed they are referring to these things – how to do leadership well. However, when we write about 'performing leadership' we are not interested in these things – in how to become a leader or what leaders do. Instead, what we want to do is to build on our insights from the previous chapter on the linguistic turn to look at what the language of leadership does. By 'performing leadership' what we mean is that we are setting out how simply using the word 'leadership' (and other associated words) is a kind of performance – a performance that has various effects in and of itself.

Put differently, we are relying on one of the central insights to come from the 'meaning as use' and 'ordinary language' philosophers: that words 'do' things. Of course, any so-called 'leader', however she gets defined, does things in the normal sense of the word. However, our focus in this book is on the language of leadership, and how simply using terms like leader and leadership does things in the sense of changing social relations. Using the labels 'leader' and 'leadership' has consequences in ways that bear comparison with the Pygmalion effect and our insights about the broader topic of discourse.

In corporate life, the word 'leadership' is woven into our shared cultural fabric in the same way that we find other words whose meanings we might also sometimes want to surface and challenge, for instance 'team'. All of us will probably have been part of a team that was a team in name only – where there was an uneven distribution of effort, power and resources, and where rewards and credit for success (or blame) were not shared equally. In such situations we may have been cynical about the label team. At the same time we perhaps recognized that it can be useful corporate language because, as a euphemism, 'team' helps to gloss over imbalances of power and an unequal sharing of resources and rewards. Using the word 'team' in this context takes us a step further away from actively questioning these imbalances of power because it is not simply a label, but something that provides its own justification for how work is controlled.

For example, one slightly incoherent but extremely common label for a formal role is that of 'team leader'. Indeed we saw how commonplace this term has become in ordinary usage in Chapter 3. This formula mashes together two contradictory logics of coordination – collectivism and hierarchy. Needing a team leader suggests that the kind of shared purpose and common goals that a team might ideally have is not enough to organize work effectively. Instead, they have to be 'led'. This prompts a very simple but also revealing question. Is the team leader (who would typically be paid more, be able to exert more formal power, with greater access to and more influence over more senior colleagues) a leader or are they a team member? There is a tension between the vision of a team as people united in shared purpose, and the reality of a group requiring supervision. Uncovering these kinds of tensions is valuable because it can tell us about the play of power in organizations.

The Virtue of Cynicism

Our focus on 'performing leadership' stems from a similar cynicism to that which people can experience when being part of a 'team'; especially when they are aware that the so-called 'team' is a team in name only. But cynicism need not be simply something that reflects disenchantment or an existential grumpiness. Instead, when scrutinizing corporate language, cynicism can become something that is more directed and purposive. One explanation for why the cynics were originally given that title is because they clung doggedly (*kynikos* – dog-like) to their beliefs, even when this ran counter to prevailing fashions and tastes. They were renowned for being shameless and even vulgar, attacking the powerful and the trappings of power.

The most famous cynic was the ancient Greek philosopher Diogenes. In what was without doubt a crowded field, Diogenes was arguably the most unconventional and celebrated philosopher in ancient Athens. He followed ascetic principles – asceticism being the belief that one could learn to survive with very little, and certainly without luxury. For ascetics, the avoidance of pleasure is itself a virtue (this is still a common theme in many of the world's major religions). Diogenes did not simply live by his own principles – which would have been challenging enough – he led his life in a way that was an example to others. This led him to reject all kinds of social conventions and to behave in ways that shocked others. Perhaps as part of his shamelessness, he was given the nickname 'The Dog' or *kynos*. He was wilfully disruptive (he sabotaged Plato's lectures) and seems to have been almost a cross between a satirist and a performance artist. Diogenes is associated with a number of images that are still striking today – one is that he lived in a barrel. Another is that he walked through the streets of Athens at daylight, carrying a lamp and claiming that he was trying to find an honest man.

We can illustrate this doggedness by sharing our favourite story about Diogenes. This is also a story about someone who unquestionably did merit the title of leader: Alexander the Great (and someone to whom we return in the next chapter). The meeting between Alexander and Diogenes is a highlight in the ancient writer Plutarch's biography *Alexander*. More than this, it is also one of the most famous stories in Western philosophy. Alexander (who had himself been a pupil of Aristotle's) came to visit Athens in search of the wisest thinkers. Plutarch describes what happened:

> Many statesmen and philosophers came to Alexander with their congratulations, and Alexander expected that Diogenes of Sinope also, who was tarrying in Corinth, would do likewise. But since that philosopher took not the slightest notice of Alexander, and continued to enjoy his leisure in the suburb Craneion, Alexander went in person to see him; and he found him lying in the sun. Diogenes raised himself up a little when he saw so many persons coming towards him, and fixed his eyes upon Alexander. And when that monarch addressed him with greetings, and asked if he wanted anything, 'Yes,' said Diogenes, 'stand a little out of my sun (Plutarch, no date).

This justly famous anecdote gives us a wonderfully human and simple way of imploding the authority of the most powerful figure (leader) in the ancient world – or perhaps the most powerful figure in the history of humanity. It is a useful model of cynicism to try to keep in mind in our own sustained attack on the language of leadership. Diogenes reminds Alexander – and his hangers-on – that however powerful he is, and however much he is surrounded by the trappings of power, he is still just a human being. The same as any other person he is a temporary barrier to the sun – and furthermore, that there is also nothing he can do for Diogenes.

When we are trying to surface some of the hidden dimensions to the use and meaning of 'leadership', we are also trying to unmask and demystify so much of what is present in contemporary corporate speak. This language gets in the way of an accurate representation of power. We want to show how that language of leadership can mean that we risk losing sight of some comparatively basic truths about the typical organization of work.

The mask created by the language of leadership leads to a false picture of corporate life – across each of the private, public and charity sectors. Nowadays, the presence of leadership language is something that affects so many people's daily experiences of work. In the pursuit of a purposeful cynicism, we are continuing with ideas that are inspired by the linguistic turn, and our understanding of the relationship between words and the world, but we are also going to focus more closely on how this applies in corporations and other organizations. Central to this then is the study of language and corporate power.

Language and Corporate Power

To recap one of the main insights in the linguistic turn, and in Table 6.2 in the previous chapter, is that we understand nowadays that labels of social phenomena are not mere description, they are constitutive (they 'make' or 'do' things). When it comes to understanding corporate language, the constitutive effect of discourse can be amplified in two ways. First, we understand from some of the earliest work informing the linguistic turn that language is a shared activity. Work organizations are communities that have typically hard boundaries that govern membership and non-membership. A great many of our experiences of organizational life, and the experience of things such as organizational culture, come about because we experience common membership. This sense of common boundaries – of who is 'in' and who is 'out' – means that there is a strong and shared platform for discourse. This shared platform for discourse is fundamental to organizational members because it reflects not just people's affiliations, but their identity.

Another insight from descendants of the linguistic turn is that language is a key basis for exercising power. This leads us to a second way in which organizations can amplify the constitutive effects of discourse. Work organizations tend to be organized in terms of a basic logic and common goals – in corporations this usually serves the pursuit of profit. Even where different members' own goals and interests diverge from the organization, there is typically a taken-for-granted consensus about the basic purpose of most work organizations. We would say that this divergence of interest is as – if not more true – when it comes to the goals and purpose of organizations in the public and charity sectors, notwithstanding that there is no profit motive.

The original insights into the linguistic turn came from considering language communities. The term 'community' was usually used to refer to a much more loosely defined network of people and texts with shared understandings and meanings: meanings and understandings that were spread across society as a whole. But the modern work organization has far greater sharpness around its boundaries and much greater consensus in terms of its core imperatives. When it comes to looking at corporate or organizational language, the power of language to do things is amplified in two ways then. First, this is because these harder boundaries reflect a sense of membership and identity of the kind that comes with a formal organization, and second it is because the basis of this shared membership is a common working logic or imperative that is quite unlike the kind of affiliations we might see in other kinds of community.

These are the sorts of effects that can be common to other kinds of groups: religions or sports clubs for example, but work organizations, particularly private corporations, are different in important ways because of their influence over so many employees' daily lives and because of the alignment of their essential logic (the pursuit of profit) with society as a whole. Furthermore, unlike in community life, within which we have considerable choices about how and with whom we engage, most of us need a job to survive. This being the case, within work organizations the power imbalance is never simply a function of hierarchy, instead the power of hierarchy is amplified by wider labour market conditions in which workers generally have less power than the organizations – and the top managers – that employ them.

Focusing on these two core ideas that apply to corporations – (i) shared community, (ii) basis for exercising power – can show us why the role of language has become so central to the study of organizations. For example, they both become relevant when understanding how new ideas and practices are disseminated and interpreted – buzzwords, management fads and fashions, say. They explain how actions and expectations are made to seem legitimate or natural and unquestioned. You might never question that you were assigned to a 'team' rather than a 'group' for instance, or why you are working in what is called a 'customer retention role' – even if in essence this means dealing with people who are closing their accounts.

The terms we use affect much more broadly how people make sense of social phenomena – explaining, for instance, why companies sometimes choose between different words for 'pay' (remuneration, reward, incentives or compensation) and 'performance' (quality, excellence, customer satisfaction, goals, targets). They are also relevant to how the practice of management is carried out – whether a role is understood as, say, 'real-time problem solving' or as 'firefighting'. When we understand language itself as a powerful resource that is a collective activity that emerges from and shapes the social world, we can quickly see the relevance of scrutinizing 'corporate language'.

The Gloomy Vision of Economics

Whilst it can be easy to be cynical about some corporate language, terms like 'team' or 'team leader', at the same time this could be criticized as being a fairly superficial target for cynicism. As we have mentioned before, terms like 'reach out' and 'touch base' or 'going forward' are easy targets. Plenty of people have written about the corrosive effects of this kind of euphemistic froth.

The roots of corporate language and its effects can be traced much deeper than mere surface effects though. To see how this might be the case, it is helpful to recall one of the insights from the linguistic turn – that labels do not merely describe they make the world. Failings and abuses of corporate language are an obvious symptom of an underlying problem, but they are only part of the picture. As well as considering these easier targets for cynicism, we also have to consider the role of research into organizations. This is because language is central in understanding the relationship between the study of management as an academic discipline, and the practice of management. As a consequence, there are uncomfortable implications for people who study and research business and organizations.

For example, when describing the legacy of what he calls 'bad management theories', Sumantra Ghoshal (2005: 76) argues that a 'gloomy vision' of management studies has been spread by business schools in particular. At the dark heart of this vision is a series of assumptions developed from within economics that have been used to model behaviour in markets. Economists have been very good at predicting behaviour by assuming that all actors are selfish and choose in a way that maximises personal benefit. Having been inspired by this kind of amoral, instrumentalist account of human behaviour, this sort of account has shaped the thinking and practice of managers, and 'actively freed ... students from any sense of moral responsibility' (Ghoshal, 2005: 76).

Working in the same tradition and line of thought, a number of writers have sought to explain the influence of 'economics language' on management studies. Famously, John Maynard Keynes (1936: 383) said that 'practical men [sic]' who believe themselves to be free of any 'intellectual influence' were in reality 'slaves of some defunct economist'. The implication of Ghoshal's work and these later writers is that economics language influences not just Keynes' practical people, but social scientists too.

The most common way this process of economics language is affecting management practice is described is in terms of one of the descendants of the linguistic turn (discussed in the previous chapter). This is the broader phenomenon of the self-fulfilling prophecy, and more specifically the 'Pygmalion effect'. Although, strictly speaking, the Pygmalion effect results in someone being seen to take on an elevated status, economics language has not had these effects on management or managers. Whereas in *Pygmalion* the flower seller is someone who goes up in the world and becomes a princess because people believe her to be one, economics language – with its assumptions of self-interested, independent individuals – has had the opposite of a Pygmalion effect. (Sometimes this is instead called a Golem effect.)

If we expect people and corporations to behave in a selfish way, and if we try to design systems to catch and punish selfish behaviour by individuals, doing so can actually create a world where everyone expects behaviour to be self-interested and where finding loopholes or ways round rules is incentivised. This gives us one example of a process where labels and descriptors shape norms, expectations and actions. In each of these examples of the relationship between management and the practice of management, there is interplay between the theories and labels used to describe social phenomena, and the effect of the use of such descriptors. Or, as we suggested earlier in the chapter, words are not just descriptions, they are 'doing' things.

To develop this idea and extend some of the themes in the previous chapter on the language of leadership, we can start to branch out from the term discourse a little further. There are two ways in which we can do this: in terms of a 'discursive practice' and the concept of 'performativity' – which is the theoretical foundation for this chapter's title of 'performing leadership'. We realize we are getting progressively more technical with these terms but doing so will help to move beyond the kind of superficial cynicism that is easy to a much deeper appreciation of the roots of corporate language.

Discursive Practice

One explanation for the relationship between economics language and corporations can be found in the work of French philosopher Michel Foucault. In his account of a 'discursive practice' (Foucault, 2002), he shows that what we might otherwise take to be knowledge, or a universal truth, is instead seen as something that is much more local and constructed in a particular context. Rather than there being any kind of transcendental knowledge or truth, a discursive practice will reflect the practices and functions of a particular community.

The idea of a discursive practice is helpful to us because it continues with one of the main themes in 'discourse': that labels also make the social world. However, it goes further by saying more about the nature of social mechanisms that support this kind of effect. A practice is something shared by a community of interest, and also specific to a certain time and place – the traditions or prevailing assumptions about how the world works, about what things are sacred or taboo.

This is a sharp contrast to the idea of scientific knowledge as shown at the top of our hierarchy of sciences in the last chapter. Instead of acknowledging progressive uncertainty and unpredictability, Foucault denies that knowledge about the social world ever has any ultimately 'real' status. Whatever it is that becomes something 'known' is always something known by a given community at a given time. It is a function of their local context and it will change as the community develops ways of representing these practices to others. The example Foucault goes into most detail on this is mental illness. What we now would call mental illness, or the names we would give to different kinds of mental illness, does not reflect the discovery of a truth about human nature. This is why he gives us a book titled *A History of Madness*. For Foucault 'madness' is not a biological or medical condition that simply exists 'out there' in the world, and about which there can be facts free of interpretation. Instead madness is a function of various social mechanisms and processes which encourage us to see it in a particular way and so in that sense, bring 'it' into being.

In the same way that madness is not a biological truth, but should be seen in terms of a discursive practice, the things we know about leadership are also similarly constructed. Our 'knowledge' of leadership reflects the prevailing customs, conventions and practices of a community. This knowledge is not the result of any kind of truth or fact or law-like rule as if we were looking at the laws of motion or the relationships between time and space. Instead the various things that we generally call leadership – the 'truths' about leadership – are merely expressions of widely taken-for-granted conventions about organizations and the wider world of business. They are 'truths' (in the plural) because in different settings and across communities and eras we will create a different, local version of 'the truth' about leadership – as products of the sorts of discourse prevailing at the time.

Importantly, just as leadership is a product and artefact of discourse and discursive practices, terms like 'leader' and 'leadership' have their own discursive effects. They take on a power and affect the social world where they are used in different settings and by different people. Calling someone, now, a leader rather than a manager, or ascribing to them a leadership role – rather than an administrative role – is not simply labelling. It has effects. Having considered the role of a discursive practice, we can extend the basic insight of 'discourse' – that describing the social world is itself constitutive – further by considering these effects.

Performativity

One of the most influential 'ordinary language' philosophers of the twentieth century was John Austin. The central insight he is credited with relates to one specific way in which language has constitutive effects. He argued that words 'do' things and the main theoretical framework he is associated with is called 'speech act theory' (Austin, 1962). Austin differentiated between performative and constative language. Performative language was that which had effects, constative was purely associated with the communication of meaning. This distinction echoes the two sets of different concerns of (i) those philosophers of language who concerned themselves with sense and reference, and (ii) those who looked at language in use.

By focusing on speech 'acts', Austin was emphasizing that in some settings simply saying words (an 'utterance') is in itself enough to bring about some kinds of change in the social world. There is not simply a (constative) conveying of meaning but there is a (performative) dimension. This is because very often when we make statements we do so following certain social conventions, and in settings or contexts that give our words an additional or amplifying effect. He gave some paradigmatic examples – such as saying 'I bet' in a casino or bookmakers, or 'I do' in a wedding ceremony, or 'I bequeath' as part of a last will and testament. Each of these has force because of its location, the timing of the utterance and social norms and expectations.

The interesting thing about Austin's extension out from these paradigmatic examples is a striking implication: that *all* utterances are in some way performative – all utterances do *something*. This implication should be easier to accept and more familiar to us if we revisit the idea that there is no neutral place to stand when communicating with others – we are always enmeshed. Remember, for instance, our example of using the term partner or wife – neither of which is a neutral descriptor (and there could not be any neutral description). It is not difficult to see that there are many examples in the workplace where someone says things that will carry extra weight because of their formal role or because of their informal sources of power.

Consider this very same comment on a piece of work: 'that doesn't look quite right to me, does it to you?' This comment could have completely different effects if it were said by a junior colleague, a close colleague, or a very senior manager, or a client. In relation to calling things leadership there are two dimensions to this performativity. First, there is the implication that by saying someone is a leader their words should then carry extra weight somehow. Second, there is the idea that simply using the label leader and the associated language of leadership directly influences a situation and set of social relations.

Though Austin did not leave behind very much written work, he has had many later champions and the idea of performativity has had a profound influence on a number of different fields and in relation to various social phenomena, notably in our understanding of gender, sexuality and race. Identities and memberships (in terms of gender, sexuality and race) are increasingly thought of as things that are performed and that become made real through interactions, rather than as being biological or social facts. State institutions or those in powerful positions can reproduce inequalities in society by 'making' people members of categories that are seen as problematic or deviant or simply less powerful.

Being a young, black male (to take one example) is not just an intersection of biological facts. From a personal perspective it can also be understood as a lived experience of belonging to different categories (youth, blackness, maleness) or some combination of those categories. At times, age could be more important to one's identity and self-expression than gender, but then the combined membership or the intersection of ethnicity and gender might be more important to one's sense of self than any one of these categories in isolation. In other words, willingly taking on and embracing membership of some kind of category could be an individual expression of who someone is as part of a personal project of giving one's life meaning – what could be called 'self-identifying'.

On the other hand though, the actual lived experience of belonging to these different categories might be at times something that is neither chosen, nor a result of self-identifying. Instead, a person's belonging to different categories could be experienced by being subjected by others to the meanings they give to those categories. If the combination of being young, black and male is more typically seen by a state agency (social services, policing, mental health) to represent a 'threat' or a 'risk' then people who are young, black and male may have more negative encounters with the police or social services, or mental health agencies. This could lead to examples of the Pygmalion, or perhaps more accurately, the Golem effect.

The benefit of drawing on speech act theory is that it helps us to see one way in which our social identity can be something that is not just a given – like the kind of 'fact' of being in a particular role. Instead, who we are is brought into being as people interact with others and with institutions. Speech acts are a way to understand how membership and social identity are 'performed': made real through discourse because when we use words these words 'do' things. They can label us as being members of categories that are understood by others to be 'normal' or 'deviant', as 'ordinary' or 'special' or perhaps as more or less important or powerful or prestigious and so on. Because of the constitutive aspect to discourse and mechanisms like the self-fulfilling prophecy these labels have real-world effects.

Performativity and the Language of Leadership

Where this becomes relevant to the language of leadership is there are nowadays so many mediums and opportunities for people to name themselves (or others) as leaders. This readymade language is a taken-for-granted feature of many work organizations, but it also influences language in other organizational settings – such as schools and voluntary organizations. Calling someone a leader 'does things' because it is a marker of a category membership. Moreover, while leader is for many an aspirational or somehow 'special' title, calling one person a leader does not just affect their work experiences, it affects how others relate to them. This is because we automatically think of leaders as being in a two-way (or dyadic) relationship with their followers.

Terms for minority groups – particularly those that are used as insults or to convey imbalances in power or status – often have a silent, implied dyadic relationship. This is because they are understood as being in contrast to a more powerful majority group. When people use 'queer' as a form of hate speech they do not need to express the majority category 'straight' or 'normal' because this is already implied by the term queer. Interestingly, these insults become less powerful once we open up this silent category of the implied majority group. This is because we begin to see that the majority is not homogenous but is itself made up of other groups. There is no one group who are 'normal'. Sexuality can be understood as a continuum for instance. Also many people who would call themselves 'straight' would be left out of the implied hate speech majority category because they have no problem with other people's sexuality.

The attribution of 'leader' is both less subtle and also more dangerous in some ways than calling someone queer might be. It is less subtle because we readily understand that naming someone a leader only makes sense if they have a follower, or – more typically – several followers. The reason it is potentially more dangerous is that whereas using hate speech is abhorrent to most people and readily criticized, the term leader is seen as an unequivocally necessary and – almost always – a good thing (as we show in more detail in the next chapter). As we have said, there seems to us to never be any question as to the need for leadership. There is also no considered alternative to 'leadership' – it might be good or bad – but either way, it is what we unquestioningly should have. We might have incompetent or bad leaders, but the need for there to be a leader is simply a given.

PART III
The Seductions of 'Leadership'

8

THE ATTRACTIONS OF BEING (CALLED) A 'LEADER'

Having set out our theoretical stall, as it were, in the last couple of chapters we now turn to some of the attractions of being called a leader in the light of these theories. These are attractions particularly associated with the performativity of the term 'leader'. While 'manager' (at least since the industrial revolution) has tended to mean simply someone who organizes or is in charge, 'leader' is replete with many cultural connotations and different shades of meanings. Furthermore, while as we saw in Chapter 3, the cultural resonances of 'manager' are strongly industrial and work-related in tone, the word 'leader' can plausibly be applied in a far wider range of contexts. What is important to restate is that, at least until recently, its much broader cultural connotations were not primarily industrial or commercial or organizational; in everyday speech they can often not even be work-related at all. Perhaps most importantly however, 'leader' almost always enjoys positive cultural associations, regardless of the context of its use. To be called a leader these days is inevitably flattering to the person who gets to be called a leader.

The Blanket Positivity of Leadership

Such blanket positivity goes some way to explaining the term's ideological flexibility and its ease of appropriation. Whatever your particular view of life, some version of leadership will most likely be attractive to you. 'Leader' gets used across the political spectrum. For example, just as military officers are well known for both claiming and prizing a status as leaders, people called leaders are also highly valued by some groups on the radical left. (We should not forget that Orwell's satire on Napoleon the pig's leadership in *Animal Farm* was an attack primarily on Joseph Stalin.) These radical groups include many people espousing certain versions of feminism (as we shall see in

Chapter 10 there is an influential set of movements calling for women's 'leadership' in corporate settings) and by other groups who we would not, ordinarily, think of as valuing order in society in anything like the same kind of way as the military are traditionally assumed to do.

In order to illustrate how disparate ideological causes can apparently unite under the banner of leadership, let us compare the version of leadership found in the booklet *Serve to Lead* (a guide currently given to all trainee British Army Officers at their training centre, Sandhurst) with what Paulo Freire has to say about 'revolutionary leaders' in his neo-Marxist classic, *Pedagogy of the Oppressed*. First, here is what Field Marshal Sir William Slim has to say about leadership:

> We do not in the Army talk of 'management', but of 'leadership'. This is significant. There is a difference between leadership and management. The leader and the men who follow him represent one of the oldest, most natural and most effective of all human relationships. The manager and those he manages are a later product, with neither so romantic nor so inspiring a history. Leadership is of the spirit, compounded of personality and vision: its practice is an art. Management is of the mind, more a matter of accurate calculation, of statistics, of methods, timetables and routine; its practice is a science. Managers are necessary; leaders are essential (Sandhurst, 2017: 11).

Next, here is what Paulo Freire has to say about revolutionary leaders:

> [H]uman beings in communion liberate each other. This affirmation is not meant to undervalue the importance of revolutionary leaders but, on the contrary, to emphasize their value. What could be more important than to live and work with the oppressed, with the 'rejects of life' with the 'wretched of the earth'? In this communion, the revolutionary leaders should find not only their *raison d'être* but a motive for rejoicing. By their very nature, revolutionary leaders can do what the dominant elites – by their very nature – are unable to do in authentic terms. Every approach to the oppressed by the elites, as a class, is couched in terms of ... false generosity ... But the revolutionary leaders cannot be falsely generous, nor can they manipulate. Whereas the oppressor elites flourish by trampling the people underfoot, the revolutionary leaders can flourish only in communion with the people (1970/2017: 106).

While there is a lot of apparent similarity in the way the term 'leader' is used by the two authors, there is, naturally enough, a catch. We can only assume that what Freire's revolutionary leaders might actually do would, in practice, be more or less completely different to what military leader-officers would do. The fact that they have a shared rhetoric is interesting and significant; if also potentially confusing. For example, both versions of leadership appear to have in common the idea of service to a collective (though service to a collective when constructed as 'the men who follow him' would doubtless turn out to be rather different from service to a collective when constructed as 'the oppressed').

Nevertheless, and in spite of the contradictions involved, echoes of both Freire's and the Field Marshal's ideas about leadership can be detected in many of today's popular ideas about organizational leadership. Take for example, what Simon Sinek, the best-selling leadership author (e.g. Sinek, 2014), tweeted on 6th February 2018:

> Management is the practice of manipulating people for personal gain. Leadership is the responsibility of inspiring people for the good of the group.

Defining leadership in the sort of way Sinek does, as 'the responsibility of inspiring people for the good of the group' would doubtless find approval from both Field Marshal Sir William Slim as much as it would from Paulo Freire. Furthermore, if managers were to be seen as the equivalent of Freire's 'elites' (both Freire's 'elites' and Sinek's 'managers' are said to manipulate others) then Freire would doubtless join Sinek in their vilification. Just like Sinek, we might note, the Field Marshal is also less than complimentary about managers. In any event, Freire, Sinek and Field Marshal Slim would be at one in seeing their version of the leader as an unconditionally good thing; a view that is shared, presumably, by the many thousands of people who have retweeted or 'liked' Sinek's tweet.

The observation that when different people talk about 'leaders' they may simultaneously be conjuring up entirely different images and ideals is an important one to which we shall return later in the chapter. For now, however, we want to suggest that the fact that the term 'leader' is widely seen as an unconditionally good thing is, at least in part, a reflection of the dominant ways in which, throughout history, the term has been used. As we show next, with the possible exception of views about Nazis in World War II (the term 'Führer' is [or perhaps better, *was* – it very rarely gets used any more] the German word most frequently translated as 'leader'), the term has almost always been associated with what is taken to be 'the good'. This is the case, even though what counts as 'the good' can, in practice, mean radically different things to different people and groups. Nevertheless, in today's society as throughout most of history, it is very difficult indeed to use the term 'leader' without it having positive connotations – including when the term is being used in its most basic and empirical sense: as merely the one in front.

The Leader as the One in Front

At its most apparently simple and empirical a leader is someone (or something) who is, literally speaking, at the front. The leader of a race is the one who is in front of the others; a market leader in dishwasher tablets tops dishwasher tablet sales; the leader board lists those with the best scores – and so on. In a race, it is worth pointing out, the leader has followers, but only because they are – again in the most literal of senses – behind the leader. In other words, there are plenty of contexts in which we commonly use the term 'leader' (and indeed 'follower') where there is no implication of any direct influence by the leader on their followers, or vice-versa. What is being referred to by the term leader can often simply be the fact that someone is in the leading (i.e. usually the front) position.

However, even in these sorts of contexts, being called the leader is never *just* about being in front. This is because if we talk about the one at the front as the leader we are implicitly saying that we think that to be at the front is valuable in some way. In other words, it is always a good thing to be the leader, *by definition*. This is because, unlike in a race, where being at the front is always a good thing, there are plenty of situations in which being at the front is of no particular significance. In such cases, the person who happens to be in front would not be called a leader.

Take, for example, someone sitting at the front of a classroom of students simply by virtue of their surname beginning with an 'A'. The student who gets to sit at the front because of an arbitrary convention would not be referred to as the leader of the class. There are also situations where a position at the front can be an actively bad thing. Think, say, of the company that has the highest accident rate in the country. Such a company would hardly be called a 'leader in accident rates', except perhaps with deliberate and cruel irony. Just like the student whose name begins with an 'A', the reason why this company would not be called the leader is because appearing at the top of such a list would not be valued (to say the least). On the other hand, it would make sense to call the company with the lowest accident rate a leader in accident prevention.

Being at the front – when being at the front is valued in some way – seems to be at the root of most other ways we can plausibly use the term leader. A 'leader' in a newspaper is the article we turn to first because it is the prized spot for the best journalist to demonstrate their skills. In the theatre, leading women and leading men are the ones who are the stars of the show. As in the case of the race, there is no particular implication that they are influencing other members of the cast to be better in their roles; merely that they are the most prominent actors in the performance and that this prominence is highly valued in the context of the theatre.

Being at the front – when being at the front is valued – seems also to be at the root of how we have come to use the term 'leader' in organizational life. As we shall see however, being at the front in organizational life has, over the years, come to be associated with other ideas – especially: (i) influencing others (not merely having followers behind you but *actively influencing* these followers), and (ii) the idea that leaders have an unusual ability to deal with complex, 'strategic' ideas.

To chart the history of these associations we look at three domains of leadership. First, we suggest that ideas about leadership started with the military; in fact, with the armies of classical Greece. Second, we move to the world of political leaders – links between military leaders and political leaders are close because through most of history military and political leaders were more or less inseparable. Third, we move into an area that might seem at first glance much more remote from these two as we examine some of the counter-cultural leaders of the 1960s – whom we call 'hippie leaders'.

Military 'Leaders': Leaders with Literal Followers?

The archetype for all subsequent leaders was Alexander the Great – the figure blocking Diogenes' sunlight we met in the last chapter. Since Alexander, many kings and noblemen, and more recently military officers, have traditionally been portrayed as leaders of armies and navies. The basic reason for them being portrayed in this way seems likely to be because, historically speaking, military commanders were traditionally leaders in the literal sense we've just discussed. They were leaders in that they were positioned at the front of their armies as they went into battle. Rank-and-file soldiers were followers also in the literal sense that they were traditionally positioned behind the leader. The term 'leader' has stuck until today, even though nowadays the most senior military 'leaders' tend to be a very long way indeed from the front of any actual battle. For instance, George II personally led troops at the Battle of Dettingen in 1743, thereby becoming the last British monarch to (literally speaking) lead his troops into battle.

Importantly however, a battle is self-evidently not a race. In a race, as we have seen, leaders are not thought of as directly influencing followers in any way. In a battle, by contrast, the very act of putting oneself at the front or 'in the lead' (and therefore potentially in the most vulnerable position) has, in itself, traditionally been assumed to be inspirational to the rank-and-file; a necessary prerequisite for achieving mass participation in the battle. Officers who are believed to get soldiers to follow them – not just in the literal sense of having the ordinary soldiers positioned behind the officer but in getting them to do things by being in the lead that they would not have done without such inspiration – have long been widely represented as leaders; leaders in the sense of influencers of those who follow them.

For a modern take on this belief, let's turn again to the British Army's current guide for its officers, *Serve to Lead*, where we can find comments such as the following:

> Infantry section and platoon commanders must possess the minds and hearts of their soldiers. Strength of character is not enough. Successful leadership in battle, although complex and intangible, always seemed to me to depend on two factors. Firstly, soldiers must have confidence in their leaders' professional ability and, secondly, they must trust them as men. It helps, too, if a leader has the reputation of being lucky (Sandhurst, 2017: 11).

Indeed, some of the earliest scientific studies of leadership (i.e. when this sort of influencing phenomenon starts to be represented specifically as leadership in psychology) were of military officers. According to Sheffield (2000: 42), quoting F.C. Bartlett's 1927 book *Psychology and the Soldier*:

> Leadership is the phenomenon that occurs when the influence of A (the leader) causes B (the group) to perform C (goal-directed behaviour) when B would not have performed C had it not been for the influence of A; the influence of A being generally welcomed by B.

We had to read this quote a few times too! But it shows that (even in a military context) leadership is essentially understood as influencing (rather than ordering) people to do something they would not otherwise have done, but welcome doing.

This sort of assumption about the nature of leadership is one which is echoed across many definitions of organizational leadership – including the basic definition by Grint – 'having followers' that we quoted earlier. Indeed, it is relatively uncontroversial to claim that many of the traditional ideas about the personal influence, and the otherwise inspirational nature often claimed for people represented as (civilian) organizational leaders are lifted, more or less, directly from the military use of the term.

The military source of such ideas about leaders is, we suggest, a particularly powerful one in terms of why the notion of leadership has had such an impact on the wider culture, including on organizational life. Books and comics, war films and many other similar cultural media glorify the figure of the military officer. Similar portrayals of military officers go back at least to stories of Greek heroes like Odysseus, Achilles, Ajax, Hector, etc. Their (legendary) involvement in the siege of Troy represents some of the earliest accounts of people who (were their roles translated into today's terms) we would most likely think of as military officers. One thing all these sorts of stories did for the hero–officer–leader was to mythologize his (it was always *his*) heroism. Not only did he seem pivotal in saving the world as we know it, his prowess generally extended into his personal, often including his sexual, successes. As Keith Grint et al (2017:15) argue, the term leadership is 'throbbing and overflowing with (eroticized) meaning'.

Of the many similar figures from war films we could mention in this context is Douglas Bader. He is particularly memorable for us in the context of military officers, not least because the 1957 film about his life, *Reach for the Skies*, is still shown regularly on British television. Bader was an historical figure, a Royal Air Force (RAF) officer who flew fighter aircraft during World War II. What was remarkable about him was that he managed to overcome the amputation of both legs following a pre-war plane crash in order to defend his country as a fighter pilot, and yet he still went on to become one of the war's most successful RAF pilots.

There is of course a much darker side to military leadership which we shall turn to in a moment. It has to be said, however, that for many people (perhaps especially men, and including those who have had nothing to do with military life) the figure of the military officer and the ideals he is portrayed to embody are attractive and powerfully inspirational. The ideals and virtues represented in so many films and earlier stories and legends have influenced the ways in which many of us might like to be able to think of ourselves. We have little doubt that the strong, deeply historically embedded and probably inescapable cultural associations between the figure of the leader and the figure of the military officer have much to do with the popularity of leadership in today's work organizations. It is surely significant, for example, that so many textbooks on organizational leadership are typically peppered with often rather shallow references to idealized military figures: Napoleon, Nelson and so on. Grint's *The Arts of Leadership* is a notable counterpoint to these superficial treatments of the military as it is both historically accurate and in depth. Sinek too is more sophisticated than most when discussing leadership lessons from the US Marine Corps.

Even if these kinds of figures are portrayed in accurate terms however (and they rarely are in most writing about leadership), it seems to us extraordinarily tenuous to believe anyone working in a civilian job can draw practically useful lessons from such figures. The life-and-death situations of warfare are thankfully very far away from the relatively mundane sorts of circumstances most of us find ourselves in at work. Additionally there are vast differences in terms of how hierarchical an organizational setting the military undoubtedly is, and always has been. There is surely at least a deep irony – if not an outright contradiction – in drawing on these settings and at the same time emphasizing how leadership involves followers' freely-given consent.

Lions Led by Donkeys

Across the world and throughout history, military officers have almost universally required strict and unquestioning obedience to their orders down a chain of command; especially, though not exclusively, in times of war. Indeed, for people like Field Marshal Slim to imply that the 'leader and the men who follow him represent one of the oldest, most natural and most effective of all human relationships' – and that leadership so defined is the principal way in which the military is run – seems to us romantically aspirational at best, if not naïve or even deliberately misleading. During World War I, for instance, the British Army court-martialled some 200,000 soldiers, about 20,000 of whom were found guilty of offences carrying the death penalty (albeit the death penalty was only actually carried out in 309 cases).

World War I may have been an extreme example, and we would not want to claim that in the heat of battle military officers *never* inspire 'other ranks' to acts of bravery that they would not have performed in any case. On the other hand, it is clear that in practice (and in spite of the self-serving rhetoric of leadership) even in battlefield conditions, large numbers of soldiers do in fact disobey orders as the figures for the court martials in World War I suggest. Or, to put it another way, an officer is far from being the inspiring leader of every soldier formally under his (or very latterly her) command.

Tens of thousands did willingly sign up during World War I and, in effect, were marched to their deaths through obeying what, with hindsight, were insane anachronistic orders based on outdated technologies. Furthermore, of course, soldiers are dealt with very harshly for not following orders, should they get found out. When push comes to shove in the military, obedience to orders down a rigid chain of command trumps any romantic notion of leadership as freely-given consent. Hence the phrase 'lions led by donkeys' became particularly resonant in the war's immediate aftermath.

Such strict discipline may well be necessary in times of war. Arguably though, given that strict discipline always trumps inspiration and leadership, the rhetoric of leadership seems rather self-serving. The kind of rhetoric Field Marshal Slim uses can be read as an attempt to write out any account of the disobedience of many soldiers and the ruthless punishment meted out in response. Indeed, what seems to have happened is that the military is the source of modern ideals about leadership but that in its transfer into ordinary work organizations, many of the things that the military can take for granted (such as the authority to lock up or even kill those who mutiny) cannot be part of most work organizations. What is left, therefore, is an imagined ideal which bears little relationship to what most of us experience.

There are of course, plenty of other critical things that can be said about military authority being represented as leadership. For example, this particular idealization of the leader almost always and necessarily involves a certain denigration of the follower (see Chapter 9 for more on this theme). In the case of the military officer as leader, the implication seems to be that his followers, the rank-and-file soldiers, would be less likely to fight, or at least would fight less enthusiastically without an officer's leadership. But this sort of implication is surely an insult to other ranks. Many such other ranks clearly 'hate officers' – as Burt Lancaster's character Sergeant Milton Warden famously put it in the 1953 Hollywood movie *From Here to Eternity*. Nevertheless, as the same film shows, other ranks are perfectly capable of acts of extreme bravery without recourse to any leadership from officers. For instance, officers hardly feature in the film's portrayal of the defence of Pearl Harbor against the unexpected Japanese attack.

Another point that is often made is that a very apparent and overt heroic masculinity is inherent within the figure of the military officer. This masculinity is something that is surely obvious from the multitude of popular images of military officers that many of us have. These are images that typically involve hyper-masculine Hollywood actors like Errol Flynn, John Wayne, Clint Eastwood or Tom Cruise in epitomizing military officers through their film roles. Arguably, similar forms of heroic masculinity, with their roots in the military, are subtly reproduced in today's corporate life. Indeed, many commentators see such phenomena as important factors underpinning the still shocking relative absence of women from the most senior jobs. This is a problem that is likely to be one that is only exacerbated when people like CEOs and military officers both get represented in the common rhetoric of leadership – with all its constitutive, performative effects.

Furthermore, if figures like Clint Eastwood and Tom Cruise playing military officers are inescapably tied up with the leadership mystique, then this clearly marginalizes femininity's role in what these portrayals encourage us to think of as 'leadership'. Indeed, these figures hardly leave much room for LGBTQI people either; and for that matter, neither do they leave room for anyone who doesn't have white skin. Indeed, Helena Liu's and Christopher Baker's recent analysis suggests that, '"doing leadership" is inextricably linked to "doing whiteness", while the invisible presence of whiteness in leadership discourses sustains white power and privilege' (Liu and Baker, 2016: 420).

Possibly less widely discussed are the implications of idealized military leaders for our understanding of the related idea of social class – especially the relationships between social class and formal authority. Ideals based implicitly on military leaders can subtly shape our ideas about gender, sexuality and ethnicity in relation to anyone else who gets represented as a leader. In the same way, idealized images of the military officer also tend to naturalize the superiority of what can still intelligibly be called (at least in the UK) the 'officer class'.

To explain what we mean by the 'officer class' here is an excerpt from the journalist Blake Morrison, who is writing in the *The Guardian* newspaper about his encounters with British military officers on the battlefields of the Iraq War in 2003:

> Major General Robin Broms, Group Captain Al Lockwood, Brigadier Andrew Gregory and their colleagues on the front line – they seem so terribly upper, or at any rate upper-middle ... Sandhurst [the training centre for British army officers] has created a new generation of officer toffs – or 'tofficers'. Among the most impressive is Colonel Chris Vernon, who has a habit of carelessly rubbing the back of his neck while assessing the battle ahead: 'We don't underestimate the task in hand, but we've a degree of confidence in ourselves.' Indeed, yes. With his unruffled innocence, Vernon is the kind of handsome, strong-jawed officer who used to zap Nazis in schoolboy comics. No less of a surprise than the rise of gentleman commanders has been the admiration that they have occasioned in the media. Supporting the troops is one thing; eulogising their bosses another. To judge from the press they have had, you would think our army officers were saints, not military line-managers (Morrison, 2003).

In order to make his critique more stinging, it seems to us that Morrison quite deliberately deploys terms like 'bosses' and 'line-managers' in this context of military officers. These terms have the effect of subverting and undermining the kinds of platitudes about leadership in the army we quoted earlier by Field

Marshal Sir William Slim. In the Field Marshal's account, you will recall, leadership was emphatically *not* management. Nevertheless, in the same way that people like CEOs get glamourized when we talk about them as leaders, we think the jobs of military officers can also do *without* the glamourization that the term leader lends it. In this sort of context, we enjoyed the comment made by Keith Grint et al (2017:15):

> We are socialized into consuming images and narratives of heroism-leadership in a way we are not with management. *Lord of the Rings* re-written as a tale of a competent manager designing an efficient and lean transportation system to dispose of a ring of untold power … would not make for as intriguing a plotline, perhaps.

However, Morrison's remarks about mainstream newspapers apparently viewing the 'tofficer' nature of officers as natural – or at least not worthy of comment – are also telling. In the UK, as is the case in most other parts of the Global North, people who have enjoyed the benefits of a private education are hugely over-represented in senior corporate jobs, and their place as the 'leaders' of industry is often seen as the natural place for such people to be. However, it seems to us to be yet another deep irony for the rhetoric surrounding the language of leadership, that while both military officers and corporate CEOs like to be called (and like to think of themselves as) 'leaders' – at the same time, many also seemingly like to present themselves and enact identities as elites. As members of this elite they are radically different from (and might be seen, conventionally, as superior to) their rank-and-file, supposed followers.

It is worth contrasting the situation in the mainstream military to the one that George Orwell portrays in his book *Homage to Catalonia*. Orwell's critique of leadership that we have already cited from *Animal Farm* comes not merely from his political beliefs, but also from his direct experience of fighting in an anarchist, non-hierarchical army during the Spanish Civil War:

> The essential point of the system was social equality between officers and men. Everyone from general to private drew the same pay, ate the same food, wore the same clothes, and mingled on terms of complete equality. If you wanted to slap the general commanding the division on the back and ask him for a cigarette, you could do so, and no one thought it was curious. In theory at any rate each militia was a democracy and not a hierarchy. It was understood that when you gave an order you gave it as comrade to comrade and not as superior to inferior. There were officers and NCOs, but there was no military rank in the ordinary sense; no titles, no badges, no heel-clicking and saluting. They had attempted to produce within the militias a sort of temporary working model of the classless society … In a worker's army discipline is theoretically voluntary. It is based on class-loyalty, whereas the

discipline of a bourgeois conscript army is based ultimately on fear ... When a man refused to obey an order you did not immediately get him punished; you appealed first to him in the name of comradeship. Cynical people with no experience of handling men will say instantly that this would never 'work', but as a matter of fact it does 'work' in the long run (Orwell, 1938/2000: 28–29).

World Leaders: The Leader as Strategist

As well as military officers, another conventionally attractive group of people whom we have long routinely talked about as 'leaders' are senior politicians and other national rulers of various kinds (see Chapter 3). That military and political figures have both been referred to as leaders is hardly surprising from a historical perspective. Until the eighteenth century and the rise of modern forms of democracy in Europe, there would have been little meaningful distinction to be drawn between someone whom we might refer to today as a senior politician, and someone whom we might nowadays call a military commander. For example, New York is called New York because the head of the Royal Navy when the colony was captured by the British in the middle of the seventeenth century was James Duke of York, brother of the then King, Charles II. Even some relatively modern figures who widely get represented as archetypal 'leaders' – such as Winston Churchill or Franklin D. Roosevelt (not to mention Adolf Hitler or Joseph Stalin) – were very close to being military figures; at least in the sense that what they are most widely remembered for is being world leaders during times of war. In effect, they too commanded armies.

One of the things that the most senior commanders of the military were traditionally supposed to do – in addition to inspiring their troops by leading them into a battle – was to set the strategic goals of the war. That is, to decide whether or not to go to war in the first place; and, having decided upon war, to determine its overall objectives. This is a role that today, at least in democracies, is one that is reserved for elected politicians. Furthermore, in modern times 'strategy' has lost most of its specifically military resonances, and has come to be applied to long-term planning more generally. *Any* decision (not just a military one) that involves new policy direction or that has complex and controversial implications tends to get represented as a strategic decision. Strategic decisions are matters which, at the level of the State, it is proper for politicians to decide upon, rather than officials, whether it be a military or civilian matter.

In other words, as we said in Chapters 3 and 4, we believe it is sensible to call senior politicians 'leaders' because what they do conforms to traditional and long-held ideas about leaders; as such it is unlikely to have perverse effects. Although they might no longer literally lead troops into battle, senior politicians have nevertheless retained one of the traditional tasks of such a leader – that of taking the really big 'strategic' decisions. Importantly, senior politicians are conventionally not supposed to be overly concerned with the implementation of strategy. Implementation (often referred to as management) is traditionally supposed to be a lesser task; something for civil servants and others to worry about.

Modern world leaders are not just strategists however. The growth of democracy that was occurring at around the same time as they were losing their role of literally leading people into battle meant that politicians can now lay claim to a new kind of more metaphorical follower, by which we really mean a new source of legitimacy: those who elected them. In other words, world leaders, such as presidents and prime ministers, can plausibly lay claim to being leaders in two well-established and traditional senses: in the sense of having followers – the electorate who can always unseat them if they are no longer a particular politician's followers – and in the sense of taking the really big strategic decisions that can directly affect all of our daily lives.

In this context, it is interesting to note that James MacGregor Burns's (1978) classic book, *Leadership* was almost exclusively about political leadership. This is the book that gave the world the idea of transformational (and transactional) leadership that has been so enthusiastically taken up by business executives since the 1980s. While it is doubtless possible to draw wider lessons from it, there is only a single chapter in the 530-page book – 'Group Leadership' (1978/2010: 287–307) – that is not explicitly about politicians. The chapter begins: 'The leader can be central to the cohesion and viability not only of nations and armies, but of smaller more ordinary groups' (1978/2010: 287). Even in this chapter, however, corporations and other work organizations hardly get an explicit mention at all.

It seems unlikely that the figure of the senior politician or world leader will ever be, culturally speaking, as overtly attractive (or as erotically charged) as the figure of the military officer might typically be. While both groups share an overwhelmingly affinity with male elites, one of the reasons for their relative lack of attractiveness is that world leaders are rarely as conventionally heroic as military officers. This is because, not least, they tend to be middle-aged, if not elderly, by the time they achieve such high office, and are seldom involved personally in heroic life-and-death situations. More importantly, world leaders, being politicians, are typically connected to ideologies that just as many people are likely to be repulsed by as they are attracted to.

Politicians also tend to be defined and remembered more by the mistakes that damaged their reputation than by their successes. Take for example the cases of Bill Clinton (former US President) and Tony Blair (former UK Prime Minister), whose terms of office overlapped during the late 1990s. Clinton's leadership will perhaps always be linked more with the name Monica Lewinsky and the sex scandal that ensued from his illicit relationship with her, than it ever will be with any of his political reforms, however successful they might (or might not) have been. Similarly, Tony Blair's misjudgements over the Iraq War continue to haunt his reputation as a world leader, some fifteen years later.

Still, at least while they are in office, world leaders probably wield more raw power than any other group on the planet – regardless of how posterity comes to view them in the end. From that point of view alone, they are surely a prestigious and attractive group whom many others would wish to emulate, or at least to be thought of as similar to. It is hardly surprising, therefore, that as early as the 1950s some writers on organizations were explicitly attempting to link the figure of the world leader to that of the corporate executive, especially in terms of the belief that the work of both groups could be characterised as the 'doing of strategy'. For example, in his classic book *Leadership in Administration*, Philip Selznick (1957: 37) claims:

> It is the function of the leader-statesman – whether of a nation or a private association – to define the ends of group existence, to design an enterprise distinctively adapted to these ends and to see that that design becomes a reality. These tasks are not routine; they call for continuous self-appraisal on the part of the leaders; and they may require only a few critical decisions over a long period of time.

It is unsurprising, therefore, that bodies like the World Economic Forum (WEF) with its annual meetings in Davos (which the US President along with other world leaders typically attends) deploy the rhetoric of the leader to refer to people like CEOs. For instance, the WEF website says that it 'engages the foremost political, business and other leaders of society to shape global, regional and industry agendas' (World Economic Forum, 2018). Indeed, figures like Clinton and Blair were among the first senior politicians who regularly used the term 'leader' to refer to CEOs. In so doing, they might be read to be signalling their support for business elites – arguably at the expense of other groups such as trade unions. As we write, in Donald Trump we have the latest and perhaps the starkest example so far, of a business 'leader' conquering the political sphere. For a recent critical take on Davos see Anand Giridharadas's (2018) book *Winners Take All*.

Leadership as New-Age Inspiration: Hippie Leaders

While it tends to deploy ideas drawn both from the older military and political domains discussed above, there is another highly distinctive genre of leadership writing which is much more personal. This is related directly and intimately to the individual; not primarily to the organization for which they happen to work. It is a genre that suggests the process of becoming a leader necessarily involves a deeply personal, almost existential voyage; one in which the leader (albeit perhaps with followers) journeys towards fulfilment and authenticity. The genre is very widespread today, but it is perhaps most notably typified in the foundational work of the late leadership scholar and guru, Warren Bennis (1989). As he famously put it: 'Becoming a leader is synonymous with becoming yourself. It is precisely that simple, and it is also that difficult.'

Read today, this sentiment sounds almost like a religious prophecy. Some people evidently find it very inspiring though; and yet to us it seems as elusive as it is obvious. In what sense, for example, is it 'difficult' to 'become yourself'? In any event, Bennis's pronouncement is perhaps the most famous example of many other popular claims about the personal, experiential and inspirational benefits of leadership. There is a plethora of books (sometimes million-bestsellers, and published by reputable publishers) which adopt this kind of tone about leadership. If you have yet to notice the books (perhaps in an airport bookstore), you may have seen brief quotes of the same sort of thing on 'motivational' office calendars perhaps, or on heavily visited websites dedicated to 'inspirational' thoughts about leadership. In fact, the site coming top of the Google list when we searched for the Bennis quote was: https://conantleadership.com/4-leadership-quotes-that-hold-us-to-a-higher-standard/. Its preamble reads:

> As leaders, and aspiring leaders, we have many constituents and they are all important. But at the end of the day you have to be able to look yourself in the mirror and feel good about what you see. First and foremost you are accountable to yourself. To be true to ourselves, it helps to discover why we want to lead, what our values are, and whether or not we sufficiently 'walk the talk'.

The site also offers an explanation of the Bennis quote used above:

> This quote is taken from Bennis' leadership book, *On Becoming a Leader*. In the same book he also writes, 'Becoming the kind of person who is a leader is the ultimate act of free will ...' He's right. We all have the capacity to do the work, and introspection, necessary to connect with our purpose. We all have the ability to channel that discovery into exemplary, integrity-laden leadership. But it is a *choice*. No-one is going to do the work for us. Bennis' words remind us that leadership, at its heart, is a noble but arduous endeavor; it's a quest to push ourselves to deeper levels of inquiry, reflection, and practice. For those driven to this leadership journey of self-discovery, the work is its own reward.

Vast swathes of writing about leadership, with the same sort of inspirational content and tone, are very widely 'liked' on social media. Many examples of the genre can easily be found, especially on platforms like LinkedIn, where managers and others with organizational roles claim to be on various kinds of personally fulfilling leadership journeys of self-discovery – as part of their job. (We examine some of these claims on social media in Chapter 9.)

It seems clear that to some extent at least, the appeal of these sorts of ideas is based upon both the military and the world-leader resonances we discussed above, resonances that invoking the term 'leader' almost inevitably create. For example, that the leader is said in the quote above to be on a 'noble but virtuous endeavor' seems to us to parallel the modern military leadership ideals we examined earlier; at the same time it also takes us back to something like medieval chivalry. Rather than the children's books and comics glorifying World War II's military officers though, the sorts of resonances invoked here seem more likely to be implicitly referencing other children's books and the films and TV shows based on them. Books perhaps like Roger Lancelyn Green's 1953 classic *King Arthur and his Knights of the Round Table* or Walter Scott's somewhat fanciful depiction of medieval England in his 1820 novel, *Ivanhoe*. In any event, rather than placing the leadership-believer in the footsteps of boring old industrialists, such idea(l)s place them firmly in the footsteps of people like medieval knights – groups who enjoy a much more illustrious and heroic ancestry.

The use of words like 'purpose' and 'quest', while further reinforcing the chivalrous and heroic resonances of the term 'leader', might also suggest that what is at stake is not merely the success of a mundane work project (March, 2005). Rather, it could start to suggest that such projects are important and significant enough potentially to concern even people of similar status to world leaders; at least in the imagination of the leader-believer.

It is rather too easy (if tempting) simply to poke fun and ridicule this genre of writing about leaders. It is tempting to poke fun at it, not least because of the potential it holds for encouraging and legitimizing multiple forms of naïve and also sometimes pretty blatant virtue signalling. Indeed more than just virtue signalling, we can see plenty of what seems to us to be obvious examples of self-deception, even outright hypocrisy based on claiming to be virtuous leaders. It also strikes us as incredibly, and at times comically, earnest. Nevertheless, we would do well not to dismiss the genre entirely. This is because many of its roots are in genuinely progressive soils; in particular, in some of the counter-cultural movements that became prominent in the 1960s. We can explain this using the idea of 'organization man'.

Organization Man

By the late 1950s, with the growth of very large organizations in both the public and private sectors that quickly occurred after World War II, especially in the US, the stultifying bureaucracy of these organizations' typically formal, pyramid-like hierarchies – along with many of their other limitations – started to become widely apparent. In his 1956 bestseller, *Organization Man*, the American journalist William H. Whyte influentially documented how those returning to ordinary life in the US after World War II had so often entered a life of drab conformity and meaningless routine, even when they had achieved senior management positions. Whyte's observations were reinforced by prominent novels and films of the era with the same kind of messages. Sloan Wilson's bestselling novel and the 1955 movie on which it was based, *The Man in the Gray Flannel Suit* for instance, or the multiple Academy Award winning film *The Apartment* (1960) both come to mind as illustrations of the futility, hypocrisy and inauthenticity encouraged by life and work in the corporations of that era (and doubtless beyond that era too).

In the context of the late 1950s and early 1960s, when many people were first discovering just how stultifying the nature of bureaucracy and managerialism in big organizations could be – and with the rise of counter-cultural movements which were, in part, a response to such perceived shortcomings – the beginnings of this more personal genre of writing about organizational leadership might well have seemed both radical and emancipatory. Indeed, the question we posed earlier: 'in what sense is it "difficult" to "become yourself"?' could have had a quite different resonance (and answer) for people who were labouring away in the offices of corporations in the 1950s and 60s than it does for many of us today.

The link between progressive social ideas and the sort of writing about leadership we are now discussing is a theme taken up by the French sociologists, Luc Boltanski and Eve Chiapello (2005) in their book, *The New Spirit of Capitalism*. For them, the qualities valued by this broad genre of leadership writing are:

> autonomy, spontaneity ... conviviality, openness to others and novelty, availability, creativity, visionary intuition, sensitivity to differences, listening to lived experience and receptiveness to a whole range of experiences, being attracted to informality and the search for interpersonal contacts (Boltanski and Chiapello, 2005: 97).

These are, as they put it, 'taken directly from the repertoire of May 1968'; May 1968 being, of course, the date emblematic of the social revolution that occurred around that time in France. It marked the start of months of social unrest, beginning with student protests against capitalism, consumerism and other traditional elite values. Though it was most dramatic in France, comparable revolutions in attitudes, especially among younger people, were evident around the late 1960s in many parts of the Global North, including in the US and the UK.

In this wider cultural context, similar ideas about leadership originating from this time – such as the thought that *anyone*, regardless of their position in the formal hierarchy of an organization, can be a leader – might have seemed genuinely subversive of the existing order, and entirely in line with the beliefs of radicals. These thoughts about the radical potential of leadership were doubtless made even more plausible by the emergence of immensely attractive, highly popular and influential figures in public life – most especially, perhaps, by Martin Luther King Jr. and Nelson Mandela, both of whom were explicitly being represented as leaders at this time.

King and Mandela were clearly progressives and self-evidently not drawn from the elite groups from which political and military leaders traditionally come. Nevertheless, they still clearly counted as leaders in many of the classical senses. They both had large numbers of willing followers and both were most certainly influencing events on a world stage, even if neither were formal political leaders in the 1960s (though Mandela was, of course, later to become President of South Africa).

Conjuring Up the Leader

We have argued in this chapter that a melee of different images and ideals are conjured up simultaneously by the terms 'leader' and 'leadership'. Some of these images and ideals will inevitably be in tension with one another. In Table 8.1 we have juxtaposed the names (and therefore implicitly the cultural images surrounding them) of some of the people who we have seen represented as leaders. We do this in order to illustrate just how different these images can be.

Perhaps more surprisingly, the variety of people referred to as 'leaders' by academics in formal, published research is almost as extensive. In their study of academic articles on leadership published in major US-based organizational journals, Mary Ann Glynn and Ryan Raffaelli (2010: 380–1):

> found an astonishing array of leaders, including Ronald McDonald ..., the Apostle Paul ..., Rumpelstiltskin ..., Mahatma Gandhi ..., Adolph Hitler ..., Rev. Jim Jones ..., Machiavelli ..., Ulysses S. Grant ..., Alan Greenspan ..., senior army officers, university presidents, country presidents, prime ministers, and CEOs.

Especially if we add to this list the rather less illustrious individuals who are also commonly referred to as leaders in organizational research – including first-line supervisors – it seems likely that all the different kinds of people who have ever been called leaders have very little in common; perhaps their differences are more important than their similarities.

Vastly different as they evidently are, the images and ideals of leaders are likely to interpenetrate and enhance one another. This is because almost all the images and ideals associated with leaders can be attractive ones – at least to some people – albeit

TABLE 8.1 People Who Some Have Called 'Leaders': Listed in No Particular Order

Alexander the Great	Martin Luther King Jr.
Angela Merkel	Robin Hood
Queen Elsa of Arendelle (from *Frozen*)	Abraham Lincoln
Mahatma Gandhi	Lt. Pete 'Maverick' Mitchell (from *Top Gun*)
Adolf Hitler	Saint Teresa of Calcutta
Mohammad bin Salman bin Abdulaziz Al Saud	Taylor Swift
Daniel (the schoolboy who sorted out shoes we met in Chapter 2)	Karl Marx
Osama bin Laden	Harry Kane
bell hooks	Kim Kardashian
Barak Obama	Donald Trump

in very different aesthetic and ideological ways. Furthermore, the variety of images and ideals available means that we can pick and choose images of the leader that suit our purposes – whether we are interested in a figure who exercises control and order, or a revolutionary. Equally we can pick leaders who suit our religious beliefs or leaders who simply seem to represent having fun. In other words, (almost) everyone can celebrate some 'leader' in one form or another. The problem is that as we each celebrate our own version of the leader we will most likely be celebrating somewhat – or perhaps entirely – different images and ideals as we do so.

What seems to be the case, however, is that the overwhelming positivity that the term 'leader' engenders tends to disguise these potentially profound ideological differences. In any event, although there are always exceptions, many leadership writers typically celebrate or otherwise refer to 'leaders' as if the figure of the leader were always a single, more or less coherent identity. In doing so, these writers, knowingly or not, can pull off a kind of rhetorical sleight of hand: anyone who likes 'leaders' (and who doesn't like some kind of leader?) will be predisposed to being sympathetic to the arguments the leadership writer presents. This is the case, even though any particular reader's image of the leader and beliefs about what a leader should be may be radically different from that of the particular writer making the claim. The language of leadership is not just rhetoric that disguises and muddies things. The fact that talk of 'leaders' is repeatedly framed in ways that have enormous appeal to influential cultural norms and values makes it difficult to think critically about leadership in any sense.

All this positivity surrounding the figure of the leader is important in the context of organizational life. What appears to have happened is that this melee of positivity surrounding the leader has slowly been appropriated by elites. As we show in the next chapter, while it is still possible to say that anyone can be a leader, it is overwhelmingly *elites* who, in practice, have become the 'leaders' in the corporate world.

9
A BOOST TO THE EXECUTIVE EGO

As we saw in the last chapter, by the 1970s, partly because of the New-Age ideas about leadership, it had become possible to loosen the strong historical links in the popular imagination between the figure of the leader and traditional military and political elites. It became plausible and attractive to imagine that someone without a privileged background – even someone working in an ordinary organization doing a mundane kind of job – might have the potential to be a leader; that they might become a bit like one of Paulo Freire's revolutionary leaders we encountered earlier. As opposed to managers (who could now start to be seen as emblematic of the old order of crushingly impersonal bureaucracy) this sort of thinking paved the way for leaders to be thought of plausibly as 'servants' or as 'authentic' or even as 'transformational' – ideas which developed in the 1970s and 1980s.

To be a manager has a certain amount of prestige attached to it, but then to call someone a 'manager' is simply to read off from the title at the top of their job description or on their office door. In contrast, to call someone a leader is more flattering because it seems to suggest something positive about the so-called leader's relationship with others. Today's language of leadership – with its emphasis on inspiring people for the good of the group (as Sinek puts it in the tweet we quoted in the last chapter) – might even seem from a superficial glance to be talking about something similar to Paulo Freire's revolutionary leaders.

Sadly though, at least in an organizational context, it very rarely, if ever, is revolutionary. This is because although some of the aesthetic qualities of revolutionary-sounding language have been retained by many of leadership's advocates, the ideological content of the 1960s student uprising – of which some of the language of leadership might remind us – has been almost entirely eviscerated and filleted. This means that today the term 'leader' virtually inevitably has problematic effects. Even an ordinary worker – whom others respect as having admirable qualities, qualities which encourage/influence others to also strive to be better — can easily get caught in a discursive web if called a leader.

This is because May 1968 was, at heart, about radical critique. It was concerned with trying to remove capitalism and its exploitation of ordinary workers by direct action. It failed to achieve these objectives, as we now know. What has happened instead, as Boltanski and Chiapello argue (2005: 97), is that its defeat has been compounded by some of its revolutionary language being placed 'in the service of forces whose destruction they were intended to hasten'. What we are left with, in other words, are 'leaders' who may well use some of the emancipatory language that echoes the aspirations of May 1968. These leaders, however, are the servants, not of the oppressed (as people like Freire would have it) but rather of capitalism and profits. Nevertheless, the incorporation of what *sounds like* the language of emancipation in the language of leadership is important to the capitalist project. It has meant that more radical ideas might *appear* to be satisfied, thereby blunting further critique. In other words, while it might seem obvious for radical groups to criticize and oppose managers, it might appear churlish, even perverse to criticise leaders, especially leaders who are widely said to be authentic or inspirational or servants or purpose-driven or compassionate or blah blah blah.

Furthermore, bosses have started to see (if not necessarily entirely consciously) how useful the term can be for enhancing their own self-image. Elite members of organizations known as leaders can narrate who they are in the particularly flattering terms that the language of leadership supplies them. They can also use it to enact new and functionally valuable workplace performances. Importantly, they can do neither of these things as effectively if they are known as 'managers.' For instance, if one thinks of oneself as a manager, the title is inescapably (and merely) a product of human and social creation. 'Leader' on the other hand suggests a characteristic that might be natural, innate and even biological. Writing in the academic journal the *Leadership Quarterly*, Jan-Emmanuel De Neve and colleagues (2013:45) seem to believe 'that leadership role occupancy is associated with rs4950, a single nucleotide polymorphism (SNP) residing on a neuronal acetylcholine receptor gene (CHRNB3).' It is hard to believe however that there would ever be a gene associated with being a manager.

In any event, it makes no cultural sense, for example, to be a 'servant manager'. Similarly, if you can think of yourself as a 'great leader' it sounds much more impressive than thinking of yourself merely as a great manager. It is hardly surprising then that today talking about bosses as great leaders is commonplace. CEOs do important jobs, doubtless; but the idea that greatness (with its intimations of transcendence and superiority) might attach to someone simply because they are a CEO is something that only seems credible, even thinkable, because of how taken-for-granted the language of leadership is becoming.

Organizational Leaders and Greatness

To examine how these processes of the enhancement of the leader might work in corporate and other organizational settings, let us start with the following excerpt from an article recently published in the highly prestigious academic journal, the *Academy of Management Review*. Here is its opening paragraph:

> History is replete with examples of leaders who are renowned for their positions of moral authority – for their status as paragons of virtue and goodness and for their ability to motivate their followers to do good deeds. Martin Luther King, Jr., worked for equal rights and inspired his followers to fight for justice, while Mahatma Gandhi emphasized compassion for the less fortunate. Winston Churchill is widely renowned for demonstrating and inspiring loyalty to the British Crown, while Mother Theresa is particularly well-known for her emphasis on the sanctity of body and spirit … Many CEOs, such as James Burke of Johnson & Johnson are admired for their care and compassion, while others, such as Whole Foods CEO John Mackey, are admired for their focus on purity. Regardless of the actions for which these leaders are most renowned (e.g., actions that reflect justice, compassion, loyalty, or purity), all of them have demonstrated an ability to leverage morality as a means of garnering commitment to a cause, tapping in to their followers' moral beliefs and conveying what it takes to be moral in a given place and at a given point in time (Fehr et al, 2015: 182).

We cannot simply let this juxtaposition of Gandhi and Churchill pass. It would seem a bizarre combination to anyone with more than a passing knowledge of British rule in India during the first half of the twentieth century. At this time, as Arthur Herman shows in his book, *Gandhi & Churchill: The Epic Rivalry That Destroyed an Empire and Forged Our Age*, Churchill opposed Indian independence (one of his ways of inspiring loyalty to the British Crown, perhaps) as vehemently as Gandhi championed it. Neither figure could plausibly be called 'paragons of virtue and goodness' – except perhaps by their hagiographers, of which both have had many.

More directly to the interests of our book however, we think it simply absurd even to consider comparing such figures with the likes of CEOs of corporations. Even though for many of us work is central to our sense of self; and even though corporate CEOs no doubt do very important and complex jobs; at the end of the day they are just doing *jobs*. Very few indeed (possible exceptions in some people's eyes might be figures like Steve Jobs or Bill Gates) are doing anything comparable to what Martin Luther King Jr. or Mahatma Gandhi or Winston Churchill did: that is, change the course of history. CEOs generally do not do whatever they do with anything remotely approaching the same kind of significance or popular support. One of the things that the language of leadership does nevertheless is that it gives such comparisons a certain kind of flattering plausibility. Calling someone like a CEO a leader is deeply flattering because the act itself invokes a whole series of positive images – including of 'greatness'. This starts to influence how everyone thinks of the so-called 'leader'; even when she is merely the CEO of a company.

Another image that invoking the idea of the leader tends to conjure up is that of someone 'good'. In the excerpt above, leaders are imagined to be 'paragons of virtue and goodness ... [with an] ability to motivate their followers to do good deeds'. As we have said, in the case of Churchill or Gandhi such assertions are highly questionable, to say the least. But a quick google of the CEOs mentioned reveals, for example, that Whole Foods CEO John Mackey has been embroiled in controversy over his attitude to health care reforms in the US, and that he has controversially strong free market and anti-union views; views which he has used his position as a CEO to express publicly. According to *The Guardian* in 2009, Mackey compared the trade union movement to herpes saying that 'it doesn't kill you, but it's very unpleasant and will make a lot of people not want to be your lover'. This statement led to calls for a boycott of Whole Foods.

It is instructive to compare the effects on Ryan Fehr and colleagues' arguments had they talked about 'managers' instead of 'leaders' in the aforementioned article. Evidently, as we suggested in the last chapter, there is much less ideological flexibility available in invoking the figure of the manager. To be sure, it remains possible to lionize or otherwise celebrate the figure of the industrial manager to some extent – as many have done in the past. Importantly, however, once we talk about 'managers' we rule out comparisons with figures like Martin Luther King Jr., or Winston Churchill. Such comparisons immediately become implausible; perhaps even impossible. This is because the wider cultural connotations surrounding the term 'manager', unlike 'leader', means that managers can never be regarded as 'great' in any sort of transcendent sense. The use of the term 'leader', in contrast, acts to lift the executive out of their relatively mundane settings and into something like the heroic; and, what is more, into doing deeds of potentially world-changing significance.

Another factor, had Ryan Fehr and his colleagues used the term 'manager', is that their ideological baggage would have been much more evident. Because of the industrial and commercial overtones of the term 'manager', it would be clearer that they were celebrating the manager from a position that actively supports the current capitalist system. However, as we saw in the last chapter, almost everyone, regardless of political allegiance or ideological preference, thinks highly of at least some aspects of Martin Luther King Jr. or Winston Churchill. The associations that come bundled with 'leader' are likely to make us think on some level about corporate bosses in the same 'good' and 'special' terms, muddying the waters when it comes to the often murky track record of many corporate bosses.

We would argue, in other words, that a key reason that the language of leadership has become popular is because, once again, it has suited the interests of those who represent corporate power – the bosses or 'capital'. This language is, in yet another way, a pro-elite resource. This resource is a kind of filter through which elites can imagine and project their identities in much more positive (and functionally useful) ways than was the case with the language of management.

Me-dership

The dominance of the language of leadership in organizational life can be seen as an example of a wider societal phenomenon of celebritization. It feeds into deeper seated myths about what success at work and in life means, and about the route to success. These are both influenced by a shared cultural image of the leader as a special individual, rather than merely as someone occupying a comparatively more senior role at work or other organization.

It is easy to see why a range of stakeholders, including those running private companies or public organizations, might want to encourage the myth that leadership means being special in some way. For example, if someone is special then this justifies their use of power. We also associate leaders with being able to build a shared vision and to provide a clear direction. What organization would not be tempted to realize these kinds of coordination efficiencies?

At the same time as leadership being seen as something for special individuals, as we have suggested, there is a massive industry that offers to sell people the recipe for becoming a leader. The idea that leadership can be bought or sold like this brings about some amusing sources of incoherence. For instance, there are courses that teach you how to be authentic – something which sounds like the epitome of fake to us. There are also courses that help you to find the 'leader within'. This sounds odd because it suggests people are like Russian dolls who on the surface are not leaders, but have a ready-formed leader inside waiting to emerge – like a miniature Clark Kent who is only in need of a phone-box. If someone did have a little leader doll inside them – or 'within' – it presumably would not be hidden meekly under layers of mediocrity. Instead it should have shouldered its way to the forefront of someone's personality structure – by virtue of having 'shown leadership' to the other parts of someone's personality.

This myth of the special individual runs in tandem with a proliferation of what we would call 'leadership chatter' on social media. Twitter, Facebook and LinkedIn are replete with 'look at me!' posts by people who are advertising their achievements and inviting others to recognize and celebrate their success as leaders. These selfie-style posts are interesting because they tell us something about how leadership is seen as a portable commodity. It is not just something carried out within an organization – because, in the main, networks on LinkedIn and Facebook are predominantly outward facing. Instead it resides within individuals, almost free of their context. They are examples, in other words, of personal projects of branding based on their self-presentation as leaders.

We do not want to be *too* critical of the people who write this sort of thing, however. After all, writing about oneself in this way also seems likely to be a response to perpetual job insecurity, and the belief that if you are well connected, even if you get dumped by your current employer, being known to others will increase your chances of not being stuck in unemployment for too long. In other words this phenomenon may well not just be ego-tripping; often it may well also be a response to anxiety.

Humble-bragging

Either way, what this kind of chatter gives us is a vision of 'me-dership'. Me-dership is what happens when people try to mimic and reflect an idealized image of a leader as a special, ascendant individual. Where people try to absorb, copy and exemplify these cultural associations of 'leadership' it shapes a particular view of work relations and a particular view of what success is. These posts often involve humble-bragging – false or incoherent claims to modesty. Humble-bragging is a particularly revealing style of communicating to consider in relation to leadership chatter – because it shows us how at the same time as craving the special status of leader, people have to deny it. This is rather like the rhetorical games played occasionally by politicians who can never openly admit to wanting to be Prime Minister (which would seem disloyal to the current PM or nakedly ambitious), but at the same time would never want to rule themselves out as a candidate. They tend to say that they would do it, almost reluctantly, if called on by their party or country.

Similarly, people practising me-dership want to associate themselves with the allure of something special and almost magical – which is the essential cache of 'leader' – but they also need to take care not to appear excessively arrogant. Their accounts often have to steer a tightrope between showing themselves to be a person who is special enough to imply that they are a leader, or that they have leadership potential, but also normal enough that their posts are not seen as wildly and ridiculously boastful.

The risk is not just one of being seen as boastful though – the greater risk is of being seen as a figure of fun. One could say that some boastfulness and arrogance is almost to be expected if we are operating at the intersection of leadership and social media. This, after all, is a world where people describe themselves in mini-biographies as 'visionary' and 'guru'. Still, a risk is that claiming the label or qualities of a leader in any straightforward and explicit way leaves one open to ridicule (for the vast majority of me-ders). This is because it could come across not just as boasting and immodest – but plain silly. Even given the proliferation of the language of leadership, to a large degree 'leader' is still something that only makes sense as a label conferred on someone by other people – their followers. When it comes to these selfie-style posts, because people are trying to establish their personal brand, their stories are self-centred and so they miss out this need for so-called 'follower' sanction and approval.

Posts on social media such as LinkedIn typically give us two stages of this me-dership journey: someone is telling the world that they are either on their way to becoming a leader, or proving that they already are a leader (see Table 9.1 below).

TABLE 9.1 Me-dership Careers

On the way to being a leader★	Proving they are already a leader★
Sharon: Growing up, I dreamt of being a pilot, or an astronaut. In school, I juggled jobs … missed lectures, but somehow was best student in my department. I'm not at the pinnacle of success yet (really long way to go) but I'm not where I used to be.	Martha: I'm sometimes asked to be a judge at an awards ceremony. It is always a delight to be asked, because it's a reflection of my profile and of the esteem in which I'm held. However on this occasion …
Shona: My 8-year old recently created a WhatsApp group on our maid's phone titled 'My new company ideas', and added his Dad and me to the group.	Craig: Wow! thank you to my 15K followers !! Numbers are not everything, but knowing I have 15,000 followers cheering me on? That is truly magical …
Mike: From the age of 18 I only ever worked 40 hour weeks. My Uni friends were partying but I put my sales career first working every weekend and late shift, hoping I would get ahead. Now at 23 I say with a great sense of achievement that I am a home-owner. In life you have to plan because it goes by quickly. Sure I have no degree but I have real experience and the real hard work starts now.	Raj: I worked my butt off. 17 hour days for 10 years to at last get to the C-suite. I was overjoyed but it isn't easy. It's a blast building super-effective teams and there's nothing better than designing a blueprint-to-customer strategy. And it is humbling to coach others so they go from good to great. But there is a downside no-one tells you about: it is lonely at the top.

★Though these are in the public domain, quotes are anonymized and some wording is altered to preserve anonymity

Sharon is humble-bragging. She says she was 'somehow' the best student – and she remains on course to dominate. Martha is invited to be judge so often it is 'always' a delight. She, revealingly, makes a narcissist's semantic slip, seeing this as 'a reflection' of her profile and esteem. The example from Shona is an interesting one because implicit in the boast about her 8-year old maid-reared child is the claim that Shona herself is a leader now. Her 8-year old, having appropriated their maid's phone, is clearly seen as on the true path to being a corporate leader. This is not even humble-bragging, but bragging-bragging. Craig's over-punctuated delight reveals the occasional absurdity of the term follower – as if every connection would even look at his posts, much less cheer each one. Mike and Raj are in a sense both virtue signalling (the virtue being hard work), and their me-dership stories are sad in different ways. Mike is on a seemingly endless, cradle-to-grave treadmill, Raj's account is not so much about how his experience has been 'humbling' but contains more examples of humble-bragging – about his ability to make good people great. It is also an echo of Orwell's Napoleon and his tough-at-the-top, burden of office spiel.

Me-dership involves a blurring of what it is to be human as people take on the meanings and identities given to success at work and try to embody them. This is less than human because these identities are interwoven with the values of corporations: profit, competition, efficiency, maximizing value and performance. When companies and recruiters seek out 'leadership skills', evidence of 'showing leadership', and a CV punctuated by 'leadership roles' they are also creating a picture of the leader as a stand-alone, portable and plug and play individual. This is a very different picture from seeing leadership as a social process that is co-created, and a product of a particular time and place.

Me-dership can also be understood as part of a phenomenon that we have already discussed – neo-liberalism. This has emerged in parallel with the rise in the popularity of the language of leadership over the last few decades. Neo-liberalism is most typically associated with taking things that were part of the public sphere or sector and turning them over to the private sector. This public/private distinction finds expression in me-dership because the values of the marketplace are what is seeping through and shaping people's identities.

Followers of the World Unite

For us, perhaps the least appealing aspect of the recent turn to leadership – both aesthetically and politically – is the practice that is inherently tied up with academic scholarship on leadership. This involves referring to people as 'followers' who ordinarily would be called something like 'workers' or 'employees'. Our ideological objections to the term 'follower' when used in this sense mirror our objections to using the term 'leader' instead of boss. We argue that both terms act misleadingly to build Santa's workshop (see Chapter 5). They construct and legitimate a workplace imagined as basically a friendly and consensual place from which all talk of conflict has been more or less excised.

To talk about 'managers' and 'workers' – the traditional terms used in this context – is, as we have already seen in Chapter 5, to acknowledge implicitly that there is a potential conflict between competing interests. For reasons we enlarge upon in this section, to talk of leaders and more specifically about 'followers' is also, in effect, to disguise, if not to deny such conflicts. In other words, just as calling managers 'leaders' is reshaping our taken-for-granted image of bosses in ways that suit elite interests, so calling workers 'followers' has the capacity to reshape our image of ordinary workers – in ways that equally suit elites.

Naturally enough, given the links between the terms 'leader' and 'follower', there are similarities when it comes to considering the effects of using the terms in leadership scholarship. In particular, just as many leadership writers claim that anyone can be a leader (regardless of their place in any official hierarchy), so it is often claimed that anyone (including a top boss) can be a follower. Here, for example, is what Mary Uhl-Bien and her colleagues have to say about the matter in their review of the followership literature published in the *Leadership Quarterly*. Their preferred view of the follower, they say:

> Does not assume that leading and following are equated with one's hierarchical position in an organization. Rather, it acknowledges that managers can also follow (and might not lead), and subordinates can also lead (and might not follow) (Uhl-Bien et al, 2014: 99).

There is a sense in which we agree with this statement — though with important caveats. It is clearly the case that senior managers can, and probably often do, 'follow' people (if you insist on using the term 'follow') lower down in the hierarchy. They might do so in the sense, for example, of deferring to a specialist with particular expertise on a specific issue. As Uhl-Bien and colleagues go on to say 'following behaviors may take the form of succumbing to the wishes or desires of another by deferring, obeying, or complying'. However, to our ears at least, to insist that these types of behaviour should be regarded specifically as 'following' seems unnatural and forced. Why not call them something like 'taking advice', say — or simply deferring, obeying or complying? We return to the significance of the unnatural and forced nature of the language of followership later in this section.

Our central point for the moment however is that, in practice (and in spite of protestations from various prominent authors) it is invariably rank-and-file workers who get to be called followers; just as it is invariably elites who get to be called the leaders. The naming of ordinary workers as 'followers' can be seen even in self-consciously 'critical' leadership research. Here, for instance, David Collinson and Dennis Tourish (2015: 590) — in an article proposing ways to teach leadership critically — seem to be saying that 'rank-and-file employees' can simply and straightforwardly be equated with 'followers':

> While many top U.S. business schools, such as Harvard, Stanford, and MIT have sessions billed as 'the view from the top,' in which 'celebrity' CEOs share their insights with students, very few courses offer a 'view from below,' in which rank-and-file employees (i.e., 'followers') of large organizations are given the opportunity to share their perspective on leadership dynamics.

We would go so far as to claim that almost all of the time, 'follower' occurs in leadership research simply because it is assumed to represent the logical corollary of the taken-for-granted assumption that bosses are leaders. If bosses are leaders then ordinary workers must be followers. Furthermore, and in spite of various calls over the years for scholars to be more discriminating in their use of 'follower', in research about leadership the term 'follower' remains more or less unexamined by those who use it as standing for something like 'junior member of staff'. In other words, Collinson and Tourish are seemingly complying with what Joseph C. Rost observes about the use of the term 'follower' in the leadership literature more generally:

> In the leadership literature since the 1930s ... followers were considered to be subordinates ... and leaders were considered to be managers... Since leaders were managers, followers had to be the subordinate people in an organization. There is no other logical equation (Rost, 1991: 107).

Uhl-Bien and her colleagues make a similar observation to Rost's. They argue that:

> The role-based, leader-centric view ... has traditionally dominated leadership research ... [and that these] role-based approaches study the follower in a hierarchical context (i.e., as a subordinate). These approaches associate leadership and followership with holding formal hierarchical positions (e.g., manager and subordinate) (Uhl-Bien et al, 2014: 89–90).

However, while there is a clear similarity between the generally unexamined and hierarchical ways in which 'leader' and 'follower' are both used by leadership researchers, there are also some interesting and significant contrasts between the cultural associations enjoyed by the two terms. For instance, as opposed to the highly positive cultural associations of the term 'leader' – which have meant that 'leader' has become popular among bosses as the term of choice to describe themselves – the cultural associations of 'follower' are almost diametrically opposed. They make it something akin to being a term of denigration. Indeed, part of our objection to the use of the term 'follower' in leadership research is a pretty basic one. It is simply that we rarely find anyone who seems to think of themselves as a follower (though we have come across people who believe that 'following' is part of 'leading'). In direct contrast to 'leader' this reluctance to think of oneself as a follower seems to hold true in more or less any work-related context. In fact, the term is hardly used except by Twitter and Instagram users (where everyone has followers) and within certain religious environments.

Even when the term 'leader' peppers company reports and government policy documents, typically the word 'follower' will be entirely absent. It is strikingly incongruous to observe how commonly the word 'follower' still occurs – *uniquely* – in academic leadership research. 'Follower' is hardly ever used by practitioners, including those practitioners who regularly refer to people as 'leaders'. In fact, academic leadership research is the only genre of organizational writing in which the term is commonly used. The relative rarity of the term in organizational life is doubtless part of the explanation, incidentally, for why it feels so forced and unnatural to talk using terms such as 'following behaviours' – especially when so many rather more obvious and natural alternative terms are so readily available.

To a certain extent, these sorts of problematic issues with the term are acknowledged by those leadership writers who still, nevertheless, promote the use of the term 'follower'. For example, Uhl-Bien and colleagues (2014: 89) argue that the 'negative connotations of the words "follower" and "following" come from the role-based, leader-centric view that has traditionally dominated leadership research'. But as explanations go, this one seems to us, frankly, little short of bizarre. As the collocations of the term 'follower' in Table 9.2 show, the dominant cultural associations of the term 'follower' are strongly related to terms like faithfulness, loyalty and dedication – which in an organizational context suggest subservience and deference.

These negative associations linked with subservience and deference which the word 'follower' has are deeply embedded in English-speaking culture. Indeed they act as a kind of mirror image when compared with the equally strong

TABLE 9.2 Word Sketch of the Use of 'Follower' in the Early 1990s and 2015: Commonest Modifier of 'Follower'

	Early 1990s	2015
1	Camp	Twitter
2	Faithful	Instagram
3	Loyal	Christ
4	Dedicated	Loyal
5	Hunt	Faithful
6	Devout	Devoted
7	Ardent	Devout
8	Keen	Avid
9	Devoted	Cam
10	Fervent	Keen

associations of dominance and supremacy that accrue to 'leader'. They are surely the kinds of factors that are much nearer the mark in explaining the negative connotations of the word 'follower' – and why we are all so reluctant to think of ourselves as followers. It seems bizarre to us to think that the negative associations have anything to do with acts or omissions on the part of leadership researchers.

Rost (1991: 107) might be a little nearer the mark than Uhl-Bien and colleagues when he says that while he himself has 'no trouble' with the word follower, 'it does bother a number of other scholars and practitioners, who view the word as condescending'. It certainly does bother us. Although we agree that calling anyone a follower is condescending (and its condescending tone is doubtless partly why so few are happy to use it to characterize their own relationship with their boss) this is not the main reason that it bothers us.

As below, we have four further problems with the use of the term 'follower' in organizations. All of them boil down, essentially, to political objections – the sort of objections that Uhl-Bien and her colleagues do not consider at all in their review of academic work on the topic of 'follower'. We argue that in a variety of different ways the term 'follower' performatively downplays and under-values the role of workers – while ignoring the extent to which there is typically conflict in the relationships between bosses and workers. It is for this reason, that 'worker' – the traditional term for rank-and-file employees in organizational life that workers use themselves often as a mark of solidarity with one another – is the term we overwhelmingly prefer and wish to defend against the potential insurgence of 'follower'.

The Flattery of 'Being Followed'

Our first objection to 'follower' is that it very much suits the interests of bosses to regard workers as their followers (even if only implicitly and without using the actual term itself). Indeed, it is not merely in their interests, it is actively flattering for bosses to believe that they have people who might be called their 'followers'. After all, there is always going to be a general feeling of personal flattery associated with the thought that people might be following you. The common sense meaning of 'having followers' presumably implies that people do what you require of them not merely out of respect for – or fear of – your *position* in the hierarchy. Rather, people do what you require because of the fact that they actively have a high opinion of *you*. In as much as they 'follow' you, they do so because of what they see as your attractively positive personal characteristics. Who, in this case, would not like to have followers? Furthermore, believing that people actively follow you – rather than simply obey you – is likely to reinforce bosses' sense of their own legitimacy. The belief that people follow you means that your decisions must be the right ones – because others have actively followed your lead. In other words, when we talk about 'followers' we are really talking about 'leaders' in a disguised manner. The only difference being that in talking about followers the leader is (self-interestedly) trying to imagine leadership from the point of view of those at the receiving end of it.

That being said, 'having followers' is an incredibly vague notion. As we saw earlier in the book, Keith Grint makes 'having followers' his most basic definition of the leader. However, if the term 'follower' can simply be equated with all rank-and-file employees then 'leader' in its turn simply becomes a synonym for manager or boss – no-one doubts, after all, that managers have subordinates. If we assume that Grint intended 'follower' to be something more than a synonym for rank-and-file employee (and presumably, he must have done) then we need some kind of criteria to answer the question 'how can I know whether or not someone counts as a follower?' The trouble is that neither Grint nor any other leadership writer we know of spells out any criteria for followers – criteria that might be used to judge in a practical sense who is (or is not) someone's follower (as opposed, that is, to being merely a subordinate).

This absence of criteria is rather convenient for bosses. 'Having followers' implies something rather special – it implies that most of us will *not* have followers. However, the lack of criteria for judging who counts as a follower means that, should a boss wish to believe that all employees are her followers, she can do so, regardless of how these employees might actually act in relation to her.

People in Organizations Are Simply Not Followers

Let us go back to the TGI Fridays case we mentioned in Chapter 4. As we saw, the company website, under the heading 'Leadership', says not only that the CEO 'is much loved, valued and respected throughout the company' but that she 'is regularly seen in the stores and will always take time with the team'. These sorts of claims are tantamount to saying that all ordinary staff members are her followers – without, of course, actually using the condescending term itself.

However, just as the lack of criteria for what counts as a follower leaves bosses free to imagine workers as their followers, it also leaves workers equally free to believe that nothing could be further from the truth. Recall TGI Fridays again – this time the letter from Lauren to the CEO. If someone were to come up with a plausible set of criteria to judge whether or not someone was your follower, these criteria could not include (presumably) factors such as say, 'having contempt for you'; 'accusing you of lying' and so on. In other words, as we mentioned earlier, we think that using 'follower' as the standard term for ordinary members of organizations is not just pro-boss, it is actively misleading. Most subordinate staff simply cannot sensibly be said to be followers in any plausibly meaningful sense of the word. To suggest that they might be – as the manner of its deployment in most leadership texts suggests – is not merely disingenuous. Most seriously perhaps it adds legitimacy and plausibility even to the sorts of ridiculous claims about being 'loved, valued and respected throughout the company' that some CEOs seem to like to make. This is the second (and perhaps the most obvious) reason why we object to the term so strongly.

Follower as a Denigrated Identity

Our third problem with the use of the term 'follower' is that there is something inherently denigrating to ordinary workers about the using the term to describe them. As we saw when we looked at the case of the military officer as leader, one of the implications of the officer-as-leader is that 'other ranks' would somehow be less courageous – or maybe would not even fight at all – were it not for the leadership of the officer. Even more importantly, however, the use of the term 'follower' implies that the identity of workers is dependent upon their supposed 'leader'. Workers, once they are rearticulated as 'followers' can easily come to be seen as the sorts of people who get their sense of self – their sense of who they are – primarily from their relationship with their boss.

Some people have argued that we should emphasize the needs of followers rather than leaders in an attempt to highlight the needs of ordinary workers over and above their bosses. However, the terminology they use confounds their intentions. When writers use the term 'follower' seemingly as an obvious, straightforward and unproblematic word for ordinary workers it is a pretty sure sign that they have entirely bought in to the readymade language of leadership. It is hardly surprising therefore, that those writers who emphasize the needs of 'followers' in organizational life, are actually (regardless of intention) making a thinly veiled call to assert the dominance of the leader. There can, after all, be no followers without a leader.

Follower Replacing 'Worker'

Our fourth objection is really the most fundamental point. It is that when people such as leadership academics use the term 'follower' what they are trying to do, in effect, is to make the word 'worker' redundant. However, we believe that it is of fundamental importance to retain the word 'worker' because of its performative role in being emblematic of working class solidarity. 'WORKERS OF THE WORLD UNITE!' is one of the world's most famous political slogans, occurring as it does in Karl Marx's and Friedrich Engels's *The Communist Manifesto* (1848/2012). Saying '*FOLLOWERS* OF THE WORLD UNITE!' reveals what a pro-boss term 'follower' is. 'FOLLOWERS OF THE WORLD UNITE!' if it makes any sense at all as a political slogan, would probably be a slogan of fascism (Adorno, 1951). The use of 'follower' is an attempt to make workers' whole identities dependent upon their (so-called) leaders.

We have shown earlier how, in virtually all organizational contexts, 'leader' and 'manager' can be used more or less interchangeably. This is because, at base, people who are called managers generally welcome being called leaders – it makes them sound more prestigious. In contrast, 'follower' is very unlikely indeed to be welcomed as a more flattering synonym for 'worker'. Substituting the term follower for worker – especially in politicized writing that takes the side of workers – reveals the conservative, pro-leader implications of the term. In order to demonstrate how different the connotations of worker and follower are we have taken the following excerpt from a newspaper article, 'Top pay in UK up by 11% as workers' wages fail to match inflation' and replaced every occurrence of 'worker' with 'follower'. It is interesting to note, in passing, that as might be expected in an article critical of bosses, they are never called leaders:

> Top pay in UK up by 11% as followers' wages fail to match inflation
>
> Pay for chief executives at Britain's biggest listed companies rose more than six times faster than wages in the wider workforce last year as the average boss's pay packet hit £3.9m.
>
> Chief executive pay at businesses on the FTSE 100 index surged 11% on a median basis in 2017 while average *follower* earnings failed to keep pace with inflation, rising just 1.7%, according to the High Pay Centre's annual review of top pay.
>
> A *follower* on a median salary of £23,474 would have to work 167 years to earn the median annual pay of a FTSE 100 boss – up from 153 years in 2016, the report showed. The gap between bosses and *followers* widened despite government efforts to hold companies accountable for runaway pay.
>
> …
>
> Rachel Reeves, who chairs the Commons business committee, said the government should take tougher measures on pay if company boards, and the remuneration committees that set executive wages, do not step in. She said: 'Excessive executive pay undermines public trust in business. When CEOs are happily banking ever-larger bonuses while average *follower* pay is squeezed, then something is going very wrong.'
>
> (Available from: https://www.theguardian.com/business/2018/aug/15/uk-top-bosses-pay-rise-average-earnings-hit-39m-2017-high-pay-centre?CMP=Share_iOSApp_Other [Accessed 15th August 2018]).

Solidarity

An important part of taking on people like CEOs, those who in a different political context might well be referred to as 'leaders', is to assert one's identity and solidarity with one another as *workers*. Furthermore, if we now look at Table 9.3 we can see a striking difference between 'worker' and 'follower'. The table shows the verbs that most commonly take 'worker' as their object (e.g. *employ* a worker), juxtaposed with the verbs that most commonly take 'follower' as object (e.g. *reward* a follower). From it we can see how the term 'worker' much more closely links to the experiences of most ordinary staff than follower does. (Please see Chapter 3 for a reminder of the corpus linguistics methods used to produce these tables.)

'Workers' are people who get sacked and fired and exploited whereas the word 'follower', in contrast, seems to take us into a non-work world of religion or (by 2015) of social media. The 2015 list also seems to hint at concerns about the rise of extremism and concerns about those who 'follow' those authoritarian style right-wing 'leaders'. Furthermore, the collocations of 'follower' in Table 9.3 seem to include more emotional relationship words, such as *encourage, persuade, help* and *exhort*. It is unsurprising then that 'follower' seems such an unnatural term to use outside of social media and religious contexts.

TABLE 9.3 Word Sketch of the Use of 'Worker' in the Early 1990s and 2015: Verbs With 'Worker' or 'Follower' as Object

	Early 1990s		2015	
	Worker	**Follower**	**Worker**	**Follower**
1	Employ	Reward	Employ	Instruct
2	Sack	Persuade	Hire	Exhort
3	Recruit	Teach	Train	Persecute
4	Train	Lead	Pay	Command
5	Pay	Attract	Protect	Devote
6	Exploit	Encourage	Unionize	Attract
7	Retire	Become	Expose	Urge
8	Hire	Help	Fire	Amass
9	Protect	Tell	Displace	Incite
10	Involve	Call	Exploit	Remind

PART IV
Resistance

10
WHAT IS TO BE DONE?

In this book so far we have argued against routinely adopting the language of leadership. We claim that it shapes, rather than merely describes organizational life, and it does so overwhelmingly in the interests of bosses and other elites. If you have agreed with most of the arguments presented in the book so far, then an obvious question arises. What is to be done?

As we have seen, today's corporate life is invariably saturated in the language of leadership. This means that on a day-to-day, practical level it is hard to avoid it, and even harder to escape it entirely. You may also be expected to go on things like leadership development programmes. What is more, at least in our experience, mundane conversations in the photocopier room or over coffee can quickly move to talking about things like the 'leadership team'; in the last few years even moans about bosses are increasingly being framed as moans about the so-called 'leadership team'.

One of us had a particularly odd experience recently that is relevant to how inescapable leadership language seems to be becoming. It was as part of the publicity for an article coming out in an academic journal published by the Academy of Management (AOM). The PR agency that the AOM uses wrote a press release about the article, and they sent a copy for approval prior to it going live. Here is an extract from the original draft of the release:

> Today, the Academy of Management, the largest global association devoted to management and organization research, published a new study that found an overwhelming number of animated Disney movies portray managers, *leaders* and everyday work life in a negative fashion. The authors believe the influence of Disney films likely shapes the way children view the working world long before they enter the workforce (Academy of Management, 2018).

It is a small detail, and one that was not really relevant to the main arguments in the particular paper in question. Nevertheless, the comment to them was that we did not mention 'leaders' in the whole article, not even once, and asked for the word to be removed. It was not removed in the final version of the press release that was sent out, however, and the agency explained the reason why they did not change it as requested as follows:

> AOM [i.e. officials working for the AOM] followed up with a comment and recommended 'I would recommend leaving in the word "leaders" since this release has a broad audience appeal, and sometimes "managers" alone is misperceived or is jargon' (Personal communication).

It strikes us as particularly ironic – and rather telling in terms of what we are saying about the current saturation of the language of leadership – that it was an official at the AOM (i.e. of the Academy of *Management*) who made this comment. We have also noticed, incidentally, that an executive committee of the Critical Management Studies (CMS) Division of the AOM, to which one of us happens to belong, gets routinely referred to in emails from AOM headquarters as the 'leadership team'. (Executive Committee is the official name of the group; and what we do, boils down essentially to organizing a stream at an academic conference.) So, in light of these subtle changes, who knows? Maybe the AOM are currently considering a name change. Perhaps before long the AOM will be the AOL: the Academy of *Leadership*?

In any event, if the language of leadership is becoming inescapable – even within an organization that has management in its name – then how, if at all, might we escape? And if we cannot escape, what can we do (if indeed we can do anything at all) as resistance?

Salvaging Something Positive From Leadership?

Perhaps the commonest response to this problem, at least among some 'critical' academics in business schools, is to acknowledge some – perhaps many – of the difficulties with the language of leadership, but try to salvage something positive from talking about leadership. In other words, their response is to reinvent leadership – to continue to use the term but to use it in ways intended to be more politically progressive than might traditionally be the case.

We can see the attraction of this course of action as at least *potentially* sensible and pragmatic. It has been said to us, for example, by someone who agrees with the thrust of our arguments in this book, that continuing to talk and write about leadership enables them to continue to influence the leadership debate – and we can see the force of this argument. We also happily acknowledge the good intentions of the people who use this sort of strategy in addressing the difficulty of what to do about the language of leadership.

The big problem with this sort of approach, it seems to us, is that the terms 'leader' and 'leadership' have become so inevitably caught up with the interests of organizational elites that simply by using the language of leadership we almost inevitably benefit these elites. This is the case, even when we are criticizing bosses but still calling them 'leaders' as we do so. Similarly when we are asserting that ordinary staff can be 'leaders', or when we are trying to make room for marginalized groups in 'leadership' positions; even then, we are still, almost inevitably, disguising power relations and subtly glamourizing those at the top of the pile.

In the light of these problems, before we outline our own preferred responses to the question of what is to be done, we discuss some of the responses of those who have attempted to retain the language of leadership to produce work that is intended to be politically progressive. We call these responses collectively 'critical leadership studies' because the phrase is becoming relatively well established, at least in UK business schools.

Critical Leadership Studies

Almost since the idea of organizational leadership was first introduced, leadership has had its critics. Exemplary work includes for us landmark papers such as James R. Meindl and colleagues' analysis of the romance of leadership, something which is: 'hinted at in the observations made by a number of social and organizational analysts who have noted the esteem, prestige, charisma, and heroism attached to various conceptions and forms of leadership' (Meindl et al, 1985: 79). It also includes Linda Smircich and Gareth Morgan's critique of leadership as the management of meaning:

> The leader exists as a formal leader only when he or she achieves a situation in which an obligation, expectation or right to frame experience is presumed, or offered and accepted by others. ... It involves a complicity or process of negotiation through which certain individuals, implicitly or explicitly, surrender their power to define the nature of their nature of their experience to others. Indeed leadership depends on the existence of individuals willing, as a result of inclination or pressure, to surrender, at least in part, the powers to shape and define their own reality. (Smircich and Morgan, 1982: 258)

Clearly then, at least since the 1980s if not before, we have been able to see that what generally gets referred to as 'leadership' in organizations tends to be bound up with insidious forms of power asymmetries, overly romanticized celebration, covert complicities and the surrender of something of oneself to the so-called leader. These features all signal leadership as a problem *in itself*, something which is hardly the mainstream view. But it is only in the last few years that critical leadership studies (CLS) has emerged as a separately recognizable approach to studying and critiquing leadership.

The emergence of CLS is closely related to the growth of the more established tradition of critical management studies (CMS). Briefly, CMS is a diverse set of ideas which, rather than being concerned primarily with increasing organizational efficiency, seeks to reveal, challenge and overturn the power relations within organizational life. This is a valuable undertaking because, in contemporary industrial societies, it is through such structures that many people are often constrained and dominated. CLS, as David Collinson argues, broadly shares CMS's political aims and intellectual traditions, but it attempts to broaden CMS's range, in that it:

> Explicitly recognizes that, for good and/or ill, leaders and leadership dynamics (defined … as the shifting, asymmetrical interrelations between leaders, followers and contexts) also exercise significant power and influence over contemporary organizational and societal processes [whereas] many CMS writers ignore the study of leadership, focusing more narrowly on management and organization (Collinson, 2011: 182).

Another feature of CLS, according to Collinson, is its emphasis on how 'leadership dynamics can emerge informally in more subordinated and dispersed relationships … as well as in oppositional forms of organization such as trade unions … and revolutionary movements' (2011: 182). We think that the prominence attached to this feature of CLS certainly reflects a critical point of view because rather than reproducing officially sanctioned corporate hierarchies it challenges and subverts them.

Indeed, work like Heather Zoller's and Gail Fairhurst's (2007: 1332) study of resistance leadership – which highlights 'the role of leadership in resisting and potentially transforming structures of domination' provides an illustration of the critical potential in such work. They provide extended examples of the leadership of dissent, focusing 'on the role of perceived unfairness and injustice as a key resource of dissent mobilization' (2007: 1340). Take this excerpt, which uses the accounts of a participant ethnography by Laurie Graham who worked in an American automobile factory. It was in this setting that Graham:

> [U]sed discourses around Japanese concepts of self-management and extant organizational policy to fight the [recently introduced and unpopular] overtime requirement. However, her refusal gains traction from other employees as it articulates simmering employee anger around this issue. Before this incident, she [Graham] describes angry reactions when the team leader asked employees to stay after shift to put away their tools because the line would no longer stop five minutes early. Employees privately complained, saying things like 'this is the kind of bullshit that brings in a union', and 'this place is getting too Japanese around here'. She says, 'From that day on, whenever the line ran up to quitting time, all of us on the team dropped whatever we were doing and immediately walked out, leaving the team leader to lock up the tools and clean the area' … That same month, after resentment grew about

the mandatory overtime, when the line kept moving after shift, 'nearly everyone on the car side put on a coat and walked out', although leaving a moving line is a cause for firing 'and everybody knew it' (Zoller and Fairhurst, 2007: 1350).

According to Zoller and Fairhurst, activists and trade unionists – among other oppositional groups – appropriate some of the influencing tools of leadership to advance causes that go against the interests of elites. It is unsurprising then, that Zoller and Fairhurst conclude by urging 'more dialogue between leadership and critical researchers in order to understand resistance leadership' (2007: 1354).

All this sort of broad conceptual discussion strikes us as absolutely fine in principle. The trouble is what happens when we examine how many CLS writers actually write *in practice*. Invariably, elites (the kinds of people who would have traditionally been called 'managers') are simply given the new title of 'leader' – even in this supposedly 'critical' work. Similarly, the kinds of people who would traditionally have been called workers are renamed followers. The very sorts of practices, in other words, we have been criticizing throughout the book are so often reproduced in CLS. It seems to us particularly insidious that the practice is still seen as relatively unproblematic by some critical academics. We would expect the language of leadership to be used enthusiastically by elites, but not by people who seem to be arguing from a similar point of view to ours. Indeed, we used an example from the work of a prominent CLS scholar, David Collinson, in Chapter 4 to illustrate some of the dangers of the language of leadership. In order to examine the issues that arise in more detail, let us turn to a small number of prominent pieces of recent CLS research.

Crossing Out Managers and Workers

We start with an article by Nancy Harding which was published in 2014 in the academic journal *Leadership*. To demonstrate how synonymous these terms really are, at least in Harding's usage of them, we have copied the article's abstract in full, and crossed out every occurrence of leadership/leader, substituting *management/ manager*; we have also crossed out Harding's follower and substituted *worker* in its place. The paper contains some very technical language and it is written for an academic audience but even so we hope you can see that no meaning is lost by swapping out leader(ship) and follower:

> This paper develops a theory of the subjectivity of the *manager* through the philosophical lens of Hegel's master/slave dialectic and its recent interpretation by the philosopher Judith Butler. This is used to analyse the working life history of a man who rose from poverty to a *management* position in a large company and eventually to running his own successful business. Hegel's dialectic is foundational to much Western thought, but in this paper, I rashly

update it by inserting a *manager* in between the master, whose approval the *manager* needs if s/he is to sustain self-hood, and the *worker*, who becomes a tool that the *manager* uses when trying to gain that elusive approval. The analysis follows the structure of Butler's reading of the Dialectic and develops understanding of the norms that govern how *managers* should act and the persons they should be. Hard work has become for *managers* an ethical endeavour, but they grieve the sacrifice of leisure. They enjoy a frisson of erotic pleasure at their power over others but feel guilt as a result. They must prove their *management* skills by ensuring their *workers* are perfect employees but at the same time must prove their *workers* are poor workers who need their continued *management*. This leads to the conclusion that the *manager* is someone who is both powerful and powerless. This analysis is intended not to demonize *managers*, but to show the harm that follows the emphasis on *management* as a desirable and necessary organizational function (Harding, 2014: 391).

As we have been pointing out throughout the book, if we call someone a 'leader' it is likely to be taken to imply that we think that there is something special about that person; that she or he is not *merely* a manager. However, in using 'leader' here, Harding is talking about a general category of person at work – it does not refer to a special individual or special relationship between that individual and someone else who follows them. It appears that she used the terms 'leader' and 'follower' simply because doing so is the genre convention required by a journal like *Leadership*. It seems very likely that we could have crossed out 'leader' and 'follower' and substituted 'manager' and 'worker' in a lot of articles in the same journal – demonstrating that manager and worker can function as straightforward replacements for leader and follower.

However, one of the reasons we have focused on Harding's work is that later on in this paper she herself explicitly makes leader analogous with manager. She also signals that the identity of the leader/manager is intimately linked with capitalism: 'it is on the body of "the leader", "boss" or "manager" that capitalism is inscribed, and it is through the leader/boss/manager that capitalism speaks' (Harding, 2014: 392). Harding also writes that 'follower/bondsman/worker' (2014: 399) are synonyms. It seems clear, too, that using leader-follower has nothing to do with the main theoretical ideas in her paper. Harding's analysis of the Hegelian master/slave dialectic via Judith Butler would 'work' using either leader-follower or manager-worker as its preferred terms.

One is left to wonder, therefore, whether the article is about 'leadership' simply because it uses the terms leader and follower. It clearly could have used manager and worker as its dominant terms. If it had done so though, even with no other changes, Harding's work would presumably have been regarded as a contribution to CMS (critical *management* studies). However, had manager been its preferred term the article would not have been published in *Leadership* because the journal requires articles to be about leaders. In other words, it seems likely that one factor fuelling the growth in the language of leadership over the last few years, at least in academic life, may well simply be the rise of journals like *Leadership*, which effectively require authors to represent their work in the language of leadership (the *Leadership Quarterly*, published from 1990, was the first major journal of this type). In any event, Harding's article is being commended as a model of writing in CLS for other leadership scholars (see for example, Tourish, 2015).

It is important to emphasize that CLS writers who nowadays prefer to talk about leaders and followers leave no doubt that they propose a critical reading of organizational life. Indeed, David Collinson and Dennis Tourish (2015) have recently provided radical criticisms of mainstream leadership research and teaching. They advance, 'the idea that leadership is socially constructed and interpreted and that "it" could mean very different things to different actors in different situations' (2015: 578). They also remind readers of 'the twin perils of hype and hubris' (2015: 580) in teaching students to be leaders, along with the need for 'the teaching of leadership … to go beyond a "rotten apple" theory of dysfunctionality and corruption to examine the barrel within which the apples have soured' (2015: 586). While welcoming and agreeing with these sorts of statements, we think the authors make an even more radical critical analysis impossible. Simply by the ways in which they use the terms, they imply that leadership and followership are neutral, natural and necessary categories of analysis. In other words, they fail to signal any reflection or reflexivity about their own use of the language of leadership.

This apparent lack of reflexivity is important, not least because many of their above critiques might be absorbed or otherwise appropriated by mainstream writers on leadership. The reason more radical possibilities for critique are important are that the mainstream can deal much less readily with the idea that its fundamental categories – leader and follower – may be interest serving *in themselves*. Unfortunately, this possibility is not – as far as we can see – even raised by Collinson and Tourish. Moreover, using the leader/follower dyad provides them with numerous problems. For example, they are right to be troubled that those involved in mainstream leadership research and teaching:

> tend to assume that the interests of leaders and followers automatically coalesce, that leadership is an uncontested form of top-down influence, follower consent is its relatively unproblematic outcome and resistance is abnormal or irrational (2015: 577).

However, they appear to overlook the possibility that at the root of the problem may lie the very terms themselves: that just by using 'leader' and 'follower' this means that interests coalesce, that consent is unproblematic and so on. As we have seen in Chapter 2, part of the general understanding of leadership in our culture includes something like 'an uncontested form of top-down influence' just as, if someone is referred to as a follower, s/he would generally be thought of as someone for whom 'any resistance is abnormal or irrational'.

Collinson's and Tourish's own formulation, 'follower dissent and resistance' (2015: 576) seems to us to crystallize the problem they have set for themselves. In what sense can a person intelligibly remain a 'follower' while at the same time displaying dissent and resistance? Someone who dissents and resists is surely (according to the connotations of the word – see Chapter 9) *not* a follower. The reader is left to try to make sense of this contradiction themselves. Perhaps they do this by concluding that in terms of their *identity* the person is always a follower – and that their dissenting and resistant *behaviours* must simply be temporary. This seems to suggest that resistance or dissent is ultimately only a form of 'helping' leaders. For us, such a conclusion is the opposite of a critical stance on the identities of workers because the leader/follower formulation implies that ultimately both leader and follower share the same goal. To avoid this problem – which one could say Collinson and Tourish have set for themselves – would be simple if they merely argued about *worker* dissent and resistance.

Unfortunately, then, by using this language of leadership, it seems to us that Collinson and Tourish also fall into the trap Mats Alvesson and Dan Kärreman identify:

> Many researchers find a market for work using the popular signifier 'leadership' because ... mainstream approaches have made leadership fashionable. Many efforts to develop 'alternative' views thus at the same time partly break with and reinforce the domination of 'leadership' ... Nuances involved in the efforts to revise 'leadership' are easily lost as the major framing reinforces a dominating 'mega-discourse,' weakening others. For example, this reinforces an understanding that the alternative to leadership is leadership, not peer relations, professionalism, autonomy, co-workership, organizing processes, or mutual adjustment offering alternative framings and understanding than what the leadership vocabulary invites (Alvesson and Kärreman, 2016: 142).

Collinson and Tourish's work reinforces an understanding that 'the alternative to leadership is leadership' by, for instance, encouraging students 'to draw on their own experiences of leadership and followership dynamics in schools, workplaces and families' (2015: 581).

To encourage such practices seems to be endorsing the use of the problematic discourse in new areas – young people's relations with one another in schools and in families. As we discussed in Chapter 2, we are particularly worried by the fact that the language of leadership is slowly percolating into schools and families. Here though, Collinson and Tourish might be read to be actively endorsing it further. They seem to end up encouraging students to see leadership and followership almost everywhere; this takes us back to our vignette about the 8-year-old Daniel and his 'showing leadership' in Chapter 2.

Collective Leadership

Another way of thinking about leadership that is often commended as a way of approaching it from a more progressive angle is to think about leadership as a collective, rather than individual practice. The phrase 'collective leadership' has now become a kind of umbrella term that seeks to capture a diversity of ideas about leadership – terms often used in this context include 'shared', 'distributed', 'pooled' and 'relational' leadership, for example (Ospina et al, 2018). While all these approaches are complex, and they can sometimes be in tension with one another, what seems to link most of them is that they all seek to turn away from an emphasis on more heroic and individualistic ideas about leadership.

It is outside the scope of our book to provide a comprehensive review of the area, but we certainly do not dismiss ideas about collective leadership out of hand. Indeed, it seems as if the basic message given out by proponents of collective leadership is that this is where to look for a radical alternative if you still find leadership attractive but think conventional approaches are uncritical. One such approach, known as leadership-as-practice, has been described in detail in a recently edited book, *Leadership-as-Practice* (Raelin, 2016a). What particularly caught our attention is that its editor, Joseph Raelin, claims that this approach, 'may, in the end, be more critical than critical leadership studies ... because it does not take as its starting point a critique of the ultimate hegemonic relation – the leader-follower dyad' (2016: 9). On the face of it at least, it seems that the book is trying to do something similar to what we ourselves have set out to do.

The basic claim for leadership-as-practice is as follows:

> The foundation of the leadership-as-practice approach is its underlying belief that leadership occurs as a practice rather than from the traits or behaviors of individuals. A practice is a coordinative effort among participants who choose through their own rules to achieve a distinctive outcome ... To find leadership, then, we must look to the practice within which it is occurring [rather than at individuals who conventionally might be ascribed leadership or followership roles] (Raelin, 2016b: 3).

The twelve subsequent chapters by a range of different authors go on to elaborate the meanings and implications of these ideas and ideals. There are some highly conceptual contributions – chapters on the philosophical bases of leadership-as-practice; its relationship to organizational democracy; its dialogical, embodied nature; its resonances and tensions with critical theory, as well as chapters more concerned with issues such as the methodologies implied by the approach (no surveys, experiments or questionnaires) and its implications for how one might do leadership development (if such a thing is still possible). Furthermore, the kinds of things discussed are neither heroic, hierarchical or instrumental. As such the accounts are a refreshing contrast with almost all the literature on leadership (including much that purports to be critical of leadership).

Even so, we do have some pretty big reservations. Most fundamentally, we wondered why it was necessary to classify the processes identified as *leadership*. This was an issue that many of the authors of individual chapters in this collected volume recognized. Nevertheless, and even though the term was far from inevitable or obvious, leadership was what these processes resolutely remained throughout the book. Yet a decade or two ago (before leadership was quite so fashionable) who knows, maybe they would have been classified as aspects of self-managed teams. In any event, why not simply see them as a necessary part of working together?

As we have argued throughout the book, the trouble is that framing issues in the readymade language of leadership (even with the various caveats and warnings that were offered in *Leadership-as-Practice*) does have effects; though we suspect that for the authors concerned, they were inadvertent effects. It was hard not to see the title chosen for the book as symptomatic of – or indeed a further naturalization of – the obsession with corporate leadership which, in part, is what our book is concerned with rendering problematic. For us, any naturalization and normalization of leadership in organizations, regardless of intentions, is intrinsically dangerous.

Unfortunately then (if perhaps unsurprisingly given the title) *Leadership-as-Practice* seems unlikely to ruffle any feathers in corporate board rooms – just the opposite in fact. There was no discussion, for instance, of leadership-as-practice implying structural change within organizations. Nor were there any examples of what we saw earlier in the chapter: Zoller and Fairhurst's (2007) resistance leadership. Surely, progressive measures like more pay for ordinary workers and less pay for executives, the removal of zero-hours contracts, etc. seem to follow logically from the desire for everyone to participate in leadership processes – and yet they remained undiscussed in the book. The picture implicitly painted by the empirical examples was of happy groups of relatively junior staff getting on with their jobs – just as their bosses, presumably, would like us to think they should.

Women's Leadership

It goes without saying that we actively welcome more women in positions of power in organizations. This is true especially at CEO level, where currently women are hardly represented at all in most industries. It seems at least conceivable, for example, that in and of itself having more women in CEO positions will make the corporations they manage a little less hostile and a little fairer to employees in minority groups. However, consistent with the arguments presented throughout the book, having more women in senior posts like CEOs should not be regarded as the same thing as having more women *leaders*. Whether we are talking about women or men, this label necessarily disguises the realities of power. It serves elite interests, and not the interests of ordinary workers, to routinely call CEOs (women or men) 'leaders'.

As male authors we are somewhat cautious about making criticisms in this area. However, we feel that a real problem for the women-in-leadership movement is that it tends to make seeking top jobs (along with providing advice to the women who are seeking them) appear to be an intrinsically progressive thing to do. As we emphasized, particularly in Chapters 4 and 5, the realities of power involved in doing a senior job, whether carried out by a man or a woman, will almost inevitably call for compromises and confrontations with workers' interests. The trouble is that you would not know this from looking at most of the blurb that promotes women-in-leadership books and courses. Yet again the language of leadership is a way of turning our eyes away from the realities of power and excessively glamourizing those in charge.

Here is a typical outline of a women-in-leadership programme, offered by a UK university. We have lightly anonymized it, though strikingly similar programmes are offered by many business schools across the globe:

Women in Leadership
On our Women in Leadership programme, you will broaden your impact and ability to influence.

Overcome the barriers to success
Today's business environment has never been more challenging for women in senior leadership roles. Working with other senior women leaders, you will learn how to leverage your personal leadership style, overcome the barriers to success and develop your career in times of change …

Who should attend
The programme is for today's female executives and those who aspire to leadership roles in both the public and private sector.

What the programme covers
The programme has been designed as one-day modules, with pre-work and inter-module work included. The core content includes:

- What is a leader?
- Emotional intelligence and trust leadership
- Values, aspirations and understanding your personal leadership style
- Small change, big impact
- Power, politics, and networking
- Culture, unconscious bias and damaging beliefs
- How to build coalitions, develop networks and make lasting connections
- Presence, influencing skills and building resilience
- Dealing with barriers
- Career progression – what do I need to do?

How you will benefit

As a participant, you will:

- enhance your power to communicate and negotiate in challenging situations
- develop your self-awareness, personal and professional development skills
- broaden your impact and ability to influence
- understand your core strengths and use them to enhance your leadership capability
- develop your personal capability to build trust and leadership
- build critical partnerships and networks

In common with standard leadership courses, there are all the usual (misleadingly) romantic, idealistic and individualistic ideas about leadership that we examined in early chapters. Indeed, some might even see this sort of programme as a way to turn women into the archetypal male leader. Although there is a brief mention of power ('power politics and networking'), it is bundled up with all sorts of other issues that draw attention away from any of the inherent problematics of power. That it is framed as leadership seems to us to be simply another example of muddying such problematics – with the (presumably desired) side-effect of making the programme more attractive to the elite potential attendees.

Instead of talking about women and leadership in this sort of context, a rather more politically progressive approach would be to follow the title of Mary Beard's recent book, *Women & Power: A Manifesto* (Beard, 2017). To talk about women and 'power' (rather than about women and 'leadership') is a more progressive thing to do because the wider cultural connotations of the term 'power' signal much more clearly its problematic dimensions (see also Tutchell and Edmonds, 2015; 2018). We acknowledge that work such as Amanda Sinclair's feminist case for leadership (Sinclair, 2014) does not downplay power. However, the wider cultural connotations of 'leadership' mean that many will assume that even feminist ideas that use the term 'leadership' will play down such problematics, if they do not hide them altogether.

Positive Cynicism

In terms of practical responses which are more in line with our preferences, there are a couple of broad options open to us. We collectively refer to them as versions of *positive cynicism*.

The first of these is to *resist* by working at a 'cynical distance' (to borrow a phrase coined in 2003 by Peter Fleming and Andre Spicer) from the language of leadership. This is, in effect, what we try to do most of the time ourselves in our own leadership-saturated jobs. The other approach (which may actually be an extension of the second) is to see the value in *reverting back* to the older, more traditional names for the things that tend to be called 'leadership' today. That is to say, seeing the value of these things when they are called 'management' but more especially when they are called 'administration'.

Working With Leadership at a Cynical Distance

We ourselves have the sorts of jobs that mean we have to be in day-to-day contact with people who frequently use the language of leadership. Of course, we are mainly talking about senior colleagues and bosses here; but even some of our regular co-worker-academics (not just the ones who specialize in leadership), along with some non-academic professional colleagues, seem increasingly to use the language of leadership. Many use the language of leadership in the sorts of mundane conversations we typically engage in at work, say over coffee.

Even in this mundane context, the language of leadership has become so normalized and internalized that at least some people seem happy to talk about their 'leader' even when they want to moan about their boss. This state of affairs is hardly surprising though, when you consider how saturated in the language of leadership even academic life is becoming – as we demonstrated back in Chapter 2. For these sorts of reasons we do not think it is feasible for us simply to ignore the language of leadership. Indeed the difficulties we are in were exacerbated because one of us occupied what our university officially called a 'leadership position' as Deputy Dean between 2011 and 2016; though funnily enough, it started out being called an administrative role until it morphed into a leadership position in 2013.

The Interview Problem

As mentioned earlier in the book, job interviews are one of the main settings in which questions about 'leadership' have become *de rigueur*, part of the taken-for-granted ceremonial of the modern interview. Furthermore, a job interview (even for an academic post) is hardly the kind of situation in which challenging the premise of a question will go down well with the interview panel. For these reasons, especially if people really want the job, they simply (and cynically) spout the sort of leader-shit expected. Both of us have (as we mentioned earlier) experienced car crashes of interviews where our answers to 'the leadership question' clearly came across as half-hearted, at best.

The interview setting also raises a broader point, with wider political – as well as personal – ramifications. Our experience of job interviews suggests in microcosm how it is much harder for there to be pluralism of belief or opinion in the neo-liberal world. Because a particular belief about leadership is now so widely established as societal truth, no other modes of being are permitted; work must be organized in hierarchical arrangements between a class of 'leaders' and a class of 'followers' – something leadership advocates, as we have seen, barely even define.

Micro-resistance

One form of resistance is, at every opportunity, to call senior people 'managers'; especially when they have a clear preference to be called a 'leader'. Some senior people in higher education really hate being called a manager – it is something they appear to consider to be almost demeaning. All the same though, in our experience at least, no one is able to insist on being called a leader. It remains a title that is conferred on people by others. We have yet to come across anyone who actually has 'leader' in their job title – though the day will surely come soon. On principle, neither of us refer to bosses as 'leaders' or to academic 'leadership' in any context outside a recruitment interview (sarcastic uses are permitted). When faced with people who believe in leader-shit, calling them a 'manager' is a great way to deflate their ego without them being able to object, at least publicly. Doing this kind of thing echoes (as mentioned in Chapter 8) the journalist, Blake Morrison, who calls military officers 'bosses' and 'line-managers' (rather than 'leaders') in his reports from the 2003 Iraq War.

We are aware, of course, that 'micro' forms of resistance are only one, personal and local way in which to challenge the dominance of the language of leadership. It would not alter the wider political effects of the language of leadership, even if we were able to change things in our own local situation. To encourage others to try and challenge the dominance of the language of leadership is, of course, one of the most important reasons for writing this book. Not only does writing a book give us licence to say what we think, it hopefully creates a space for others to resist and subvert, or simply to stay sane and distanced. If micro-resistance seems insignificant or trivial it is important to remember that what we are trying to do is challenge everyday power and the readymade uses of language.

Reclaiming 'Administration'

A related and more powerful form of resistance – one thing that anyone who holds a management or leadership position can do – is to call what they do 'administration'. This seems a useful choice for those who occupy senior jobs, but are attracted by the idea of service. To (ad) *minister* (from the Latin) is to serve; and there is, of course, no reference to leadership – or any other hint of supremacy – in the title 'administrator'. In fact, just the opposite is the case. For us, we find someone calling themselves an 'administrator' far preferable to the humble-bragging of calling themselves a 'servant leader'. It can also make them more accountable because we associate some specific virtues with effective administration such as fairness, diligence, competence, efficiency, prudence and so on. 'Leadership' is far woollier in contrast – it is as though these things are to be left to others while the leader does things that are super-ordinary and above and beyond their job.

The contrast between 'administration' and titles like 'servant leader' or 'compassionate leader' or 'humble' or 'authentic' or 'purpose-driven' leader is clear. For us, the 'servant' / 'compassionate' / 'humble' / 'authentic' / 'purpose-driven' adjectives are all undermined, or even made paradoxical, by being attached to 'leadership'. Like Orwell's newspeak which often makes opposite ideas collide with one another, each of these titles essentially says, 'I'm just a regular guy or gal, but I'm also special'. This is the sub-category of bullshit specific to leadership – 'leader-shit'. In the midst of this leader-shit, for someone relatively senior in an organizational hierarchy to self-consciously call what they do 'administration' seems important. It is much more likely to signal a genuine interest in service than anything that has leadership in the title. As far as we know, very few – if anyone at all – brags about being an administrator on LinkedIn, or anywhere else for that matter.

We have argued throughout the book that calling bosses 'leaders' and what they do 'leadership' starts to shape ideas about bosses in ways that excessively flatter and glamourize them. In the same sort of way, we believe that calling bosses 'administrators' is likely to shape ideas about them that are probably going to be more politically progressive – and in any case should bring former 'leaders' back down to earth again. Mark started his career being called an administrator in health care. When people ask him what he used to do in health care, his answer is always: 'I was an administrator'. Similarly, in our current jobs, both of us do some work that the university officially represents as 'leadership'. In spite of this we prefer to think of it as 'administration'.

Offering Answers?

Ultimately though, we cannot offer simple, straightforward 'answers' to what anyone should do, faced with a workplace saturated by terms like leader and leadership. What we hope to have done is made the case that simply using these readymade phrases has important effects. They pre-package the world in ways that flatter bosses and flatten workers, airbrushing out sources of conflict and remaking the workplace into a kind of Santa's workshop. In doing so and by calling attention to the limits and assumptions of these readymade phrases we create a space for critique as well as some validation for any feelings of cynicism readers already may have had when confronted with this 'language of leadership'.

An inspiration for us in thinking about 'what is to be done' is Michel Foucault's response when he learned of some people's reactions to reading *Discipline and Punish* (Foucault, 1991a). One of his most famous and influential books, *Discipline and Punish* gives a rich account of how power relations are expressed in organizations, taking as paradigm cases the work of prison guards and social workers. These guards and social workers told Foucault:

> The book [in part about life in prisons] is paralyzing. It may contain some correct observations, but even so it has clear limits, because it impedes us; it prevents us from going on with our activity (Foucault, 2002: 245).

Foucault responded to their concerns like this:

> My reply is that this very reaction proves that the work was successful, that it functioned just as I intended. It shows that people read it as an experience that changed them, that prevented them from always being the same or from having the same relation with things, with others, that they had before reading (Foucault, 2002: 245–6).

Foucault argues that people typically 'wish for a little monarchy' (1996: 307); that is, they want someone to guide, direct and tell them what to do. However, he resists such a role for theory: 'I am wary of imposing my own views, or of setting down a plan, or program' (2000: 154). Indeed, for Foucault, any perspective that seeks to provide us with straightforward 'solutions' is problematic:

> My project is precisely to bring it about that they 'no longer know what to do,' so that the acts, gestures, discourses that up until then had seemed to go without saying become problematic, difficult dangerous ... If the social workers you are talking about don't know which way to turn, this just goes to show that they're looking and, hence, are not anaesthetized or sterilized at all ... it's because of the need not to tie them down or immobilize them that there can be no question for me of trying to tell 'what is to be done'... the most important things is not to bury them under the weight of prescriptive, prophetic discourse ... [Critique] should be an instrument for those who fight, those who resist and refuse what is. Its use should be in processes of conflict and confrontation, essays in refusal ... It is a challenge directed to what is (Foucault, 1991b: 84).

Our own reading of Foucault's work is that, in the final analysis, resisting the language of leadership is not paralyzing (however much it might feel like that to start with). Instead, Foucault teaches us that finding ourselves in a state of no longer knowing is valuable – it forces us to look for something different. This means we can look beyond accepted ideas and conventional approaches. (For more on this kind of argument see King and Learmonth, 2015.)

In some ways this is close to the contribution of a far older philosopher, Socrates, whose style of questioning leads people to realize their errors while it shuts off any neat solutions (Morrell, 2004). Of course, we are certainly not claiming that our work is as profound or as influential as Foucault's. Still he provides an inspirational role model, and we hope that for some at least this book will have the same sorts of effects as he was pleased to see in reactions to *Discipline and Punish*. That is, we hope the book will help to unsettle habits of thought and assumptions in this readymade language. We hope it will encourage people who thought they were doing the right thing in relation to leadership to think more deeply and critically about the term itself. We also hope we can encourage some readers to think about how we might talk about things differently in the future. This, after all, is because to talk about things is also to 'do' things.

11

CONCLUDING THOUGHTS

Leadership as a Fig Leaf?

Part of what we want to achieve in writing this book is for people to stop calling bosses 'leaders' as a matter of routine. We have shown how the terms 'leader' and 'leadership' have become heavily freighted with pro-elite connotations. So much so that every time we use these terms, at least when talking about workplace elites, we are effectively casting a vote in favour of the bosses' interests – at the same time as undermining the traditional interests of workers.

The significance of each individual act is small in itself, of course. But these things soon add up. Calling things 'leadership' is essentially an act of tacit support for the current neo-liberal ideology. It has become so commonplace that the language of leadership is now built into the unnoticed and unexamined fabric of our language – and therefore into the fabric of our lives. To return to the quote from George Orwell with which we started the book: '[t]he invasion of one's mind by readymade phrases ... can only be prevented if one is constantly on guard against them' (1945/2013: 16). To avoid self-consciously speaking or thinking of senior people as 'leaders' is a significant way to resist the sort of corporate power that is increasingly invading not only our jobs, but our wider social world.

Entrepreneurship and the Language of Corporate Power

In attempting to resist corporate power, excluding other words from our taken-for-granted, readymade organizational lexicon may well be worth considering too. Leadership is not alone in rising from a relatively minor phenomenon in company practice (not to mention organizational studies) to centre-stage.

A parallel example of a similar process at work can be seen in what has happened to the fortunes of the word 'entrepreneur'. In the 1970s and before, 'entrepreneur' was a specialist term, relatively rarely used except by academics working in the tradition of the Austrian economist Joseph Schumpeter. The term was hardly uttered in day-to-day speech; not even by people who ran small businesses. Today, the term 'entrepreneur' has become commonplace – and used much more widely than simply by the people who run their own businesses.

It is not entirely surprising therefore that, nowadays, UK universities compete for a major annual prize awarded to the university judged to be the most entrepreneurial institution (see Mautner, 2005). There are also debates in parliament about making society itself more entrepreneurial, and we regularly hear calls for all of us, as citizens, to become more entrepreneurial in our daily lives. It can now even be plausibly argued that children as young as 7 or 8 should receive an entrepreneurial education. Exactly what it might possibly mean to be 'more entrepreneurial' – for a whole university as an institution, or for an 8-year-old child – does not seemingly matter. The point is (just as it is with leadership) that we all get a slice of the positivity now attached to terms that glamourize business success.

Importantly, using the term 'entrepreneur' (as opposed to 'business person') takes the focus off business per se – in just the same sort of way that the language of leadership (as opposed to 'management') does. Once the term 'entrepreneur' is invoked, gone (or so it might seem) are the boring spreadsheets and company reports, the day-to-day problems with staff not turning up to work, deliveries not arriving and so on. Calling what we do 'entrepreneurship' enables us to forget, at least for a moment, the grind and the hard slog. Talking about 'entrepreneurship' suggests instead activities that are somehow altogether desirable and romantic. Perhaps most importantly though, talking about entrepreneurship tends to make what are essentially market-based activities and processes appear more palatable to people across the political spectrum. All of us can now aspire to be 'more entrepreneurial'. In spite of the fact we might only have the vaguest idea of what it might mean, for many people it now seems quite natural and normal – and entirely positive and desirable – to want to be more entrepreneurial. Entrepreneurship seems to have become so naturalized – like leadership – that is has seemingly simply become part of the way things are.

There are doubtless other such parallels. We are suspicious of any language that is concerned with glamourizing the mundane; something which is now a widespread cultural phenomenon. Actions which seemingly help us feel better about ourselves, regardless of any substantive impact or achievement are now in vogue – even though they simultaneously engage us in more and more 'social comparison' work, which makes us feel worse, because there's always someone more 'successful' than ourselves. Arguably, in organizational life specifically, this sort of cultural phenomenon can be seen, for example, in the popularity of so-called 'positive' organizational theory (Learmonth and Humphreys, 2011) of which the celebration of leadership is doubtless a part.

We need to be particularly on our guard against the language of leadership though, not least because it is so insidious. 'Leadership' and 'leader' can trip off the tongue as a kind of reflex or habit before we have noticed these words emerge. At the same time, the idea of 'leadership' can also be very seductive. Who does not want to be able to think of themselves as some kind of 'leader' or other? In thinking of ourselves in this way, after all, we can start to put ourselves in the lineage of the many great and admirable people of the past, people who have been on all varieties of noble quests.

Perhaps most insidiously, the language of leadership can also appear to be highly progressive. It is potentially emancipatory to think, as the standard rhetoric still goes, that *anyone* can be a leader; to imagine that you do not necessarily have to occupy a formal position of authority before exercising leadership. We ourselves are not entirely denying this possibility, along with its emancipatory potential – even in organizational life – at least in theory and in the very long run. But if the 'anyone-can-be-a-leader' rhetoric is ever going to be more than leader-shit, one of the things we cannot afford to do is to carry on calling bosses 'leaders' as a matter of routine. Not least because calling bosses leaders – especially in the kind of reflex, unexamined way that is so common today – so obviously contradicts and undermines the fantasy that *anyone* can be a leader.

Future Prospects For the Language of Leadership

We should emphasize that we realize how unlikely (to say the least) it is that a significant decline in the language of leadership will come anytime soon. This was brought home to us relatively recently. For a few days during August 2018 about 11,000 fellow management academics from across the world attended the conference of the Academy of Management in Chicago. In the context of what we are trying to do in this book, some of the aesthetics of the event were (depending on how you look at it) either deeply depressing, or a reminder of just how pressing the need for a book like this is.

For instance, the Academy itself had sponsored reusable water bottles (designed, admirably enough, to reduce throwaway plastics) with the phrase 'Better world through better leadership'. A photograph of some of these flasks can be seen in Figure 11.1. They stood in rows like soldiers outside many of the rooms used for paper presentations. Surely, there can be few better symbols for the internalization of leadership than the thousands of researchers of management who internalized the water from these bottles.

At the conference Exhibit Hall – where all the major academic publishers were displaying their wares in business and management – there was a similarly depressing scene. Delegates were confronted with countless books on leadership. Invariably, these books appeared to be hymns to leadership. Not only does the number of such books seemingly rise exponentially every year, colleagues appear not only to tolerate the rise of such books, but hardly to notice it or think it in any way odd.

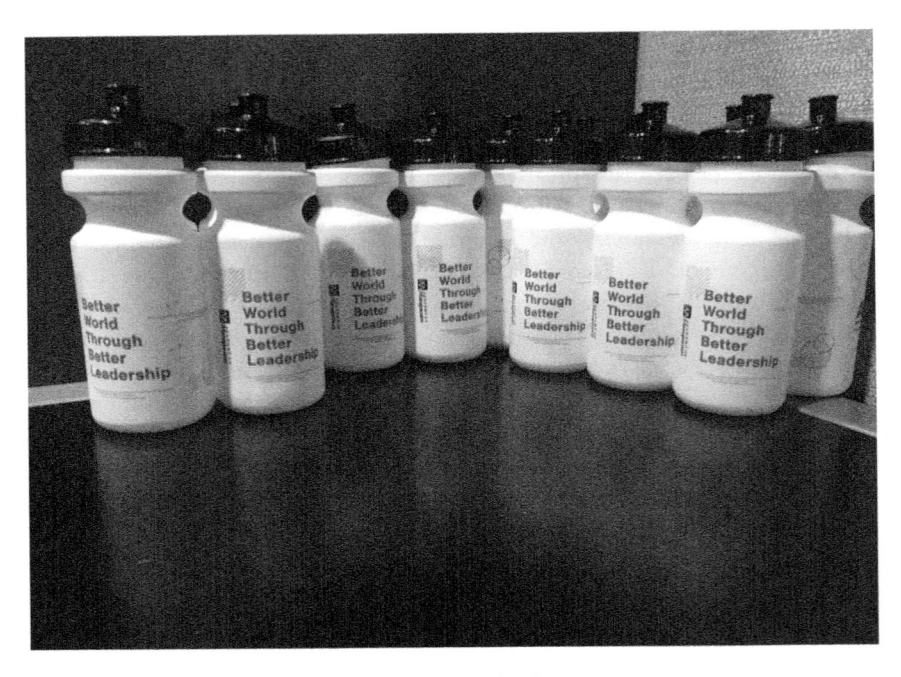

FIGURE 11.1 Better World Through Better Leadership

One of the other things making 'leadership' attractive for many of the academics who are leadership specialists is it can be a lucrative source of consultancy cash. Doing things like delivering leadership training to 'top teams', or advising CEOs on their own leadership style is a relatively easy sell for many claiming leadership expertise. Furthermore, compared to other forms of consultancy, its outcomes can be much harder to assess in terms of its direct effects on the bottom-line. Companies are particularly vulnerable therefore, to the sort of leader-shit that we have discussed throughout this book; a situation exacerbated however, by the fact that so many of the companies themselves seem to be such suckers for it. Recently, Nick Butler, Helen Delaney and Sverre Spoelstra (2018: 428) have shown how even (some) critical leadership scholars 'may end up compromising their academic values in corporate settings due to practitioner demands and other institutional pressures'. They make these compromises, at least in part, because of the earning potential provided by saying what companies want to hear in leadership consultancy.

In other words, in addition to simply keeping one's job as an expert in 'leadership', there may well be other strong incentives for academics to continue to use the language of leadership. In the same kind of way, many business executives may not happily give up the privileges of thinking of themselves as leaders – especially in the light of the fact that so many have been enjoying the benefits of the title for some years now. It will therefore undoubtedly be an uphill battle for a book like ours to be widely accepted. Still, we think it important to make our arguments and to take a stance against the language of leadership; not least because so few other people (academics or practitioners) are doing so.

Leadership as a Fig Leaf

Even if we do not find many wanting to pursue micro-resistance, we can still be optimistic about the *long run* prospects for the decline in the use of the language of leadership. Some believe that organizational leadership, at least in the sense of the worship of a heroic masculine figure, is already starting to look old-fashioned, and that it might even be little more than a passing fad. Perhaps also, there may be something just too obviously self-serving about all the pronouncements about 'leadership' made by so many highly paid executives these days. In any event, with Graham Martin, Mark has previously argued that:

> Although ... leadership is powerful, we would not suggest that merely rebranding certain practices as leadership would, in itself, transform experiences of those [junior] jobs for the better. ... Rather, should there be little substantive change in the day-to-day experiences of these staff, then simply relabelling activities under the (ostensibly positive) banner of leadership might be interpreted as a fig-leaf to hide the more oppressive aspects of life [in organizations] ... Ultimately, if the gap between everyday organizational realities and the pronouncements of policymakers does not narrow, then for all its current popularity, leadership itself may become a focus for dissent and resistance. (Martin and Learmonth, 2012: 287).

Whatever the future may hold, our book should make it easier for those who share similar views about leadership (however many there may be) to know they are not alone. It may also help others to articulate their own objections and to better discover their own modes of resistance. These can be counter projects not just to the language of leadership, but more generally to corporate power.

12
FURTHER READING

We wanted to make this book accessible to a wide audience. One of the things we have done to try to maximize its readability is to minimize the number of references to other works in the body of the main text. Though there are still quite a few references dotted throughout the book, we have borne in mind that some readers – especially non-academics – can find it distracting to plough through long lists of references. On the other hand, we recognize that many readers will want to explore the themes in this book further. Also, and as importantly, we do not want to give the impression that we are the first people to say the things we have said. Like all academics, we stand on the shoulders of many others who have written before us.

What this section is designed to do, more like an appendix than an ordinary chapter perhaps, is to supplement those references we have already provided in the text with a few others of the sort we probably would have included had we been writing a book in a more conventional academic style. Below we mention more of the kinds of sources that have informed or inspired the thinking in this book, using the part headings as a structure.

This is not an attempt to provide a comprehensive reading list on academic writing about leadership in general – or even about critical leadership studies (CLS). A good starting place for those might be the recent *Routledge Companion to Leadership* (Storey et al, 2017b) for example, though numerous other similar guides to the leadership literature are also available. For more on CLS specifically we would recommend Tourish (2013) and Carroll et al (2015).

Several recent books, like this one, are intended for a general readership who are likely to be suspicious about the virtues and abilities of 'leaders' – for instance Bloom and Rhodes (2018) and Spicer (2018). Bloom and Rhodes draw attention to the growing convergence between political and corporate leadership (we touch on this in Chapter 8). Spicer goes into the murky and unwholesome phenomenon of business bullshit. As we note, the language of leadership has contributed more than its fair share of this. An interesting book to compare ours with is Parker's *Against Management* (2002), echoed in the title we have chosen for the first section of this book. Readers may also be interested to look at Parker's (2018) latest book, which calls for business schools to be shut down.

We should also mention a few of the most recent monographs on leadership specifically, books taking a similar political stance to ours. All seek to radicalize the mainstream view, so none of the books are straightforwardly *against* leadership in quite the same way as we are. One such book is Wilson (2016). Her historical, Foucault-inflected account shows how rather different ideas down the ages about (what today we would probably call) leadership have all served the interests of elites in various ways. Another is Mabey and Knights (2018); a book concerned with equipping those with power to act ethically and responsibly – a task for which, the editors claim, conventional leadership theories are inadequate. The third book we have in mind is Spoelstra (2018). His work is unusual in leadership studies in having a firm grasp on the philosophical concepts that implicitly underpin many ideas about organizational leadership today. We must also mention a work that came out just as we were finalizing our own manuscript: Carroll et al (2019).

Part I: Against 'Leadership'

We are certainly not the first to point out the slippage between 'manager' and 'leader'. If you want to read others who have made similar points in their different ways, here is a selection: Alvesson (1996); Alvesson and Kärreman (2016); Alvesson and Spicer (2011); Brocklehurst et al (2010); Ford and Harding (2007); Ford et al (2008); Harding et al (2011); Kelly (2008, 2014); Krantz and Gilmore (1990); Learmonth (2005); McCann (2015) and McDonald (2017). As Wilson (2016) compellingly shows, a key moment in this process of slippage was the adaptation of Burns's (1978/2010) ideas about transformative leadership (originally developed to describe political leadership). The transactional elements that Bass (1985) added are clearly rooted in managerial authority (these are things like contingent reward, management by exception and so on). This meant the emergence of a 'full range' model that had both transformational and transactional elements clearly adapted for organizational managers. As Wilson argues:

> In paving the way for the ready integration of these ideas [transformational and transactional leadership from the work of Burns], Bass took it for granted that 'leadership' would be enacted by 'managers' who held positions of formal authority. Consequently, Bass's model incorporated into his conception of 'leadership' the by-then standard expectation that managers could issue rewards and sanctions to workers depending on their performance. This deliberate coalescing of the moral authority of leadership with the formal

authority of managers provided the basis for both extending managerial influence and enhancing their authority (Wilson, 2016: 135–6).

Among the earliest academics to point out the nefarious effects of what we have called the language of leadership were Gemmill and Oakley (1992). Their psychoanalytically inflected work is a major inspiration to us; as is also the more Derrida-inspired article by Calás and Smircich (1991).

We have mentioned Weber and Freud as authorities who used terms like 'leader' and 'follower' in ways we consider appropriate. Weber's idea of charismatic authority is the primary source for almost all the subsequent writings on charismatic leadership (though many writers on charismatic leadership do not appear to recognize this), and indeed, much of the work on organizational leadership in general. However, in our reading of his work, Weber sees charisma (and leadership) as the opposite of what we would expect people to have in ordinary jobs – even jobs like CEOs:

> In contrast to any kind of bureaucratic organization of offices, the charismatic structure knows nothing of a form or of an ordered procedure of appointment of dismissal. It knows no regulated 'career,' 'advancement,' 'salary,' or regulated and expert training of the holder of charisma or his aids … nor does it embrace permanent institutions like our bureaucratic 'departments' (Weber, 1948: 246).

It is in this sort of context – rather than work environments – where, for Weber (and for us), it makes sense to see the possibility of 'followers':

> Charisma knows only inner determination and inner restraint. The holder of charisma seizes the task that is adequate for him and demands obedience and a following by virtue of his mission. His success determines whether he finds them. His charismatic claim breaks down if his mission is not recognized by those to whom he feels he has been sent. If they recognize him, he is their master – so long as he knows how to maintain recognition through 'proving' himself. But he does not derive his 'right' from their will, in the manner of an election. Rather, the reverse holds: it is the *duty* of those to whom he addresses his mission to recognize him as their charismatically qualified leader (Weber, 1948: 246–7).

As for Freud, Theodor Adorno (1951) used Freud (1922) to analyze the 'erotic tie' between leader and follower – particularly in the context of Hitler and other fascist movements. More recently, Zaretsky (2018) uses Adorno's and Freud's work to examine the relationship between Donald Trump and his followers. At the time of writing it is (sadly but undoubtedly) the case that Trump has very many followers.

On so-called 'leadership' in academia, Smyth's (2017) inventively titled book, *The Toxic University: Zombie Leadership, Academic Rock Stars and Neo-liberal Ideology* is definitely worth a read.

We should say that we were more than a little reluctant to criticize Keith Grint's and David Collinson's work in the way we did in Chapters 2 and 4 respectively. Both Keith and David have clearly been influential in helping to create a space for the questioning of conventional notions of leadership to emerge. Both are obviously also alert to the problematic nature and effects of leadership discourse and practice, and neither are jumping on the bandwagon of the wider leadership industry. There is, of course, plenty of egregious nonsense being spouted by 'true believers' who love all things leadership – which we could have criticized instead. The trouble is, egregious nonsense is just too much of an easy and obvious target. Furthermore, Grint's and Collinson's work is likely to have a lot of credibility with many who are politically progressive. Indeed, we suspect that the growing acceptability of the language of leadership in some of these quarters may well have been legitimated, directly or indirectly, by their work.

Should you wish to know more about corpus linguistics (CL), Pollach (2012) provides a insightful overview of the CL method from the point of view of organization studies. Mautner (2005; 2009) provides more context and worked examples from the point of view of people interested in processes of organizing and power.

The positivity attached to the term 'leader' has been pointed out by many other authors. Perhaps the most influential of them is the article entitled 'The romance of leadership' (Meindl et al, 1985) – see Collinson et al (2018) for a discussion of Meindl et al's work.

As we briefly mentioned Duke Ellington as a band 'leader', it is worth pointing out that there is a literature on leaders in jazz. A good starting place is Humphreys et al (2012); and for a complementary take on the issue, see Griffin et al (2015a).

The kind of relationship between 'managers' and 'workers' that we argue for is really a restatement of Braverman's (1974) classic. Braverman's work in turn is a development of Marx's *Capital*. Both Marx and Braverman have been subject to much legitimate critique. Nevertheless, their central point about the structural conflicts between owners and workers remains valid in our view. It seems to us that the language of leadership is an attempt to deny this structural conflict and it is this attempted denial that is at the heart of our anxieties about the rise and popularity of the language of leadership.

Should you be interested in the notion of *hegemony*, Anderson (2017) provides a recent and very detailed account of the different ways the term has been used throughout the ages – much of which is relevant to a consideration of leadership.

Some of the links between leadership and neo-liberalism have recently been spelt out by Davies (2017) and from a somewhat different angle by Moisander et al (2017).

Finally in terms of literature supporting Part I, it is surprising, perhaps, that the explosion that we have seen in the use of the term leadership in business and management is not obviously mirrored in much of the academic research on work organizations. Putting this another way, if we are looking for someone to blame for the leadership industry and the discursive rash of 'leadership' it is not easy to blame business school research – at least not directly. The headline message, if we are looking for the language of leadership amongst academic research, is that scholars still frame their findings predominantly in the language of 'management.' A partial explanation for this could be that many of the most influential academic journals have 'management' in the title, and the leading professional academic bodies in both the US and UK do as well. As we can see from Table 12.1, both journals and these academic bodies (which have their own journals too) can be thought of as institutions – stable and enduring organizations with their own traditions and history that promote particular practices.

One can see how there could be several sources of institutional inertia in relation to journal titles. A key and most basic consideration for any piece of academic work targeting a journal is whether it will 'fit'. The title, then, is often the most succinct expression of what a journal focuses on in terms of subject area and so authors are more likely to use ways of describing their work which fit with that title, so 'management' could still hold sway. This is interesting because these kinds of institutional barriers are almost checks to the trends in everyday talk about organizations – where the terms leader and leadership seem to be replacing manager and management.

In the third column of Table 12.1, we have shown just a small sub-section (from A–C) of indicative topics that academics can study in business and management. These are adapted from the 'working knowledge' section of the Harvard Business School (HBS) website – a list of research papers and commentaries by HBS faculty. The scope and diversity of these topic areas is also very broad, broader even than the aerosol term 'leadership', and so one other reason management will remain popular is that it covers a much wider range of activities. HBS is a good source for illustrating this, because it is a very large business school, but another thing that makes this working knowledge page interesting is it is currently captioned 'Business Research for Business Leaders'.

A slight aside – as academic insiders would know – is that once a journal title is chosen there are huge disincentives when it comes to thinking about changing it. This is partly because it will result in a hit to the impact factor and citations to work in that journal. Both these are measures of how often work in a journal is referred to by other academics and they are a crucial performance indicator for any journal. With any name change comes a drop in these, because each journal name is counted as a separate entity when it comes to classification and indexing. Over a 5 or 10 year period, if the name changed part-way through and all other things stayed the same, the citations and impact factor would drop because these

TABLE 12.1 Academic Institutions with the Name 'Management' and Their Subject Areas

Institutions	Journals (journal names are in italics)	Business and Management Subject Areas (A to C)
The Academy of Management	*Academy of Management Review* (AMR) – theoretical articles *Academy of Management Journal* (AMJ) – empirical articles *Academy of Management Discoveries* (AMD) – exploratory empirical research *Academy of Management Annals* (Annals) – reviews of emerging evidence *Academy of Management Learning and Education* (AMLE) – management education. *Academy of Management Perspectives* (AMP) – more widely accessible articles	Accounting Audits; Accounting; Acquisition; Activity Based Costing and Management; Adaptation; Adoption; Advertising Campaigns; Advertising; Agency Theory; Agreements and Arrangements; Agribusiness; Analysis; Annuities; Arts; Asset Management; Asset Pricing; Assets; Attitudes; Auctions; Balanced Scorecard; Banks and Banking; Behaviour; Behavioural Finance; Bonds; Borrowing and Debt; Boundaries; Brands and Branding; Budgets and Budgeting; Business and Community Relations; Business and Government Relations; Business and Shareholder Relations; Business and Stakeholder Relations; Business Cycles; Business Divisions; Business Earnings; Business Education; Business Exit or Shutdown; Business Growth and Maturation; Business Headquarters; Business History; Business Model; Business Offices; Business or Company Management; Business Plan; Business Processes; Business Startups; Business Strategy; Business Units; Business Ventures; Capital Markets; Capital Structure; Capital; Cash Flow; Cash; Central Banking; Change Management; Change; Civil Society or Community; Cognition and Thinking; Collaborative Innovation and Invention; Commercial Banking; Communication Intention and Meaning; Communication Strategy; Communication Technology; Communication; Compensation and Benefits; Competency and Skills; Competition; Competitive Advantage; Competitive Strategy; Complexity; Conflict and Resolution; Conflict Management; Consumer Behaviour; Contracts; Cooperation; Cooperative Ownership; Copyright; Corporate Accountability; Corporate Disclosure; Corporate Entrepreneurship; Corporate Finance; Corporate Governance; Corporate Social Responsibility and Impact; Corporate Strategy; Cost Accounting; Cost Management; Cost vs Benefits; Cost; Country; Courts and Trials; Creativity; Credit Cards; Credit; Crime and Corruption; Crisis Management; Cross-Cultural and

Institutions	Journals (journal names are in italics)	Business and Management Subject Areas (A to C)
The British Academy of Management	The *British Journal of Management* (BJM) – the official journal of the British Academy of Management *International Journal of Management Reviews* (IJMR) – state of the art review articles	Cross-Border Issues; Culture; Currency Exchange Rate; Currency; Curriculum and Courses; Customer Focus and Relationships; Customer Relationship Management; Customer Satisfaction; Customer Value and Value Chain; Customers; Customization and Personalization
Other leading Academic Journals (each journal being an institution in its own right)	*Asia Pacific Journal of Management; European Management Review; European Sport Management Quarterly; Group and Organization Management; Human Resource Management; Human Resource Management Journal (UK); Human Resource Management Review; IEEE Transactions on Engineering; Information and Management; International Journal of Contemporary Hospitality Management; International Journal of Hospitality Management; International Journal of Human Resource Management; International Journal of Operations and Production Management; Journal of Environmental Management; Journal of International Management; Journal of Management; Journal of Management Inquiry; Journal of Management Information Systems; Journal of Management Studies; Journal of Operations Management; Journal of Policy Analysis and Management; Journal of Product Innovation Management; Journal of Supply Chain Management; Management and Organization Review; Management International Review; Management Learning; Management Science; Manufacturing and Service Operations Management; MIT Sloan Management Review; Omega: The International Journal of Management Science; Production and Operations Management; Public Management Review; R and D Management; Strategic Management Journal; Supply Chain Management: An International Journal; The Journal of Management; The Journal of Management Studies; Tourism Management*	

would be diluted – some being counted to the old and some being counted to the new name. One can see just how strong the disincentive to do this is because publishers make a fortune out of some of these journals and they also own the titles. To buy out a publisher and then to be able to own the journal title can cost millions.

If we look at this in a slightly more rigorous way, since the emergence of management journals in the 1950s, the proportion of empirical research that specifically uses the term 'leader' or 'leadership' in the titles and summaries of articles has remained fairly constant over time. In their comprehensive review of all articles to appear in three leading academic journals – *Academy of Management Journal, Administrative Science Quarterly* and *Organization Science* – Glynn and Raffaelli, (2010) show that overall approximately 4% of articles were empirical studies of leadership (i.e. articles that used the term leader and leadership prominently in presenting their empirical findings). They say that the frequency of these: 'peaked in the 1970s (9.18% in 1976), then declined to remain fairly steady at about 6% (or lower)' (2010: 376). More recently, the proportion of articles on leadership in these three journals did start to rise slightly in the 2000s, having risen to about 10% by 2006 (the end of the period reviewed by Glynn and Raffaelli). Broadly similar results were found by Clark et al (2014: 25) for the European periodical *Journal of Management Studies* (JMS), though JMS did not see a rise in the proportion of leadership articles in the 2000s. This is in spite of the emergence of at least one influential journal that was a natural home for papers on leadership during the 1990s (the *Leadership Quarterly*).

Such a relatively modest rise in the use of the language of leadership in academic management journals clearly does not mirror the exponential changes that appear to have occurred in many work organizations and within wider society.

Part II: 'Leadership' as Rhetoric

One of the central debates about 'science' versus the humanities in organization studies has coalesced into ideas about evidence-based management. The proponents of this approach appear to be convinced that 'science' offers the way forward in terms of making management practices better. Interestingly enough they tend to downplay – if not entirely neglect – the role of the humanities. In this debate we have tried to make as robust a defence of the importance of the humanities to organizational life as possible (Morrell and Learmonth, 2015; Morrell et al, 2015).

These chapters have been particularly strongly influenced by our reading of certain thinkers as well as those, like Roland Barthes, we specifically mention. We should draw attention perhaps to our long term interest in the work of Jacques Derrida – and that of Judith Butler, who has specifically written about hate speech (Butler, 1997). The ideas of both thinkers have directly influenced debates about performativity, which we touch on in Chapter 6.

The idea that language 'does' things to the world it supposedly merely represents – one meaning of the term performativity – is an insight, the implications of which are being hotly debated in organization studies at the moment; Gond et al (2016) attempt to set out all the debates in this area in as much of a comprehensive a fashion as possible. This particular source will also give you plenty of references on how the linguistic turn has influenced organization studies. Abrahamson, Berkowitz and Dumez (2016) have also recently set out some of the implications of performativity for an organization studies audience.

Part III: The Seductions of 'Leadership'

Much has been written about military leadership from a broadly critical perspective. For an insightful recent account with a particular sensitivity to gender, see Ashcraft and Muhr (2018). For a recent critique of something like hippie leadership see Pfeffer's (2015b) recent book. We are not particularly commending his approach, though; he does not like servant or authentic leadership but seems simply to end up recommending a different, less romantic kind of leadership.

On leaders (especially historical military leaders like Nelson or Napoleon) having hagiographies produced about them, the late James March (2018) has produced an interesting film. As the preamble puts it:

> The film uses the portrayal of leaders in *War and Peace* as a basis for raising questions about standard heroic stories of leadership. It explores some ways in which the complexities and ambiguities of history make standard narratives emphasizing the visionary role of leadership in history more mythic than real. The film explores alternative conceptions that emphasize the significance of the density of ordinary competence in organizations, the development of capabilities without clear intentions for subsequent opportunistic use, and the importance of beauty.

An important critique of followership which we should mention is that of Ford and Harding (2018) as well as the work of Blom and Alvesson (2015).

For a detailed review of all the research on what they call 'moral' approaches to leadership (i.e. authentic, servant etc.) see Lemoine et al (2018).

Part IV: Resistance

Morley (2013) provides some interesting ideas that are similar to ours about so-called 'women's leadership'. Our thoughts about reclaiming administration were inspired at least in part by du Gay (2000).

Klein (2016) has written a great book about how leadership might be emancipatory. Importantly, and the main reason we think his ideas do not conflict with ours, it is based upon fieldwork carried out primarily outside work organizations.

Should you wish to know more about the growth and impact of the term 'entrepreneurship' then Perren and Dannreuther (2012) is a good resource. If you are interested in further words likely to be associated with neo-liberalism, a good place to start would be Mould's (2018) book *Against Creativity*. His guiding idea is parallel to our own on leadership – that neo-liberal capitalism has co-opted the idea of creativity: being 'creative' now means almost exclusively to dream up new products and services for the commercial market. Indeed, the parallels between the kind of leadership we are against and the kind of creativity Mould is against are striking:

> Now, everyone is encouraged to be creative – at work, in our personal lives, in our political activities, in the neighbourhoods in which we live, in schools, in our leisure time, in the choices we make in what we eat every night, in how we design our CVs. We are bombarded by messages that by being creative, we will live better, more efficient and more enjoyable lives (Mould, 2018: 9).

Further Research Questions

To conclude, here are a few ideas for further research questions, perhaps to encourage others to continue our journey:

1. What are the wider cultural forces at work – beyond the rise of neo-liberalism – that may be behind the popularization of the language of leadership? For example, we wonder whether the bad image 'managers' generally have had to endure in novels and films over the years might be something that has led them to turn (if only sub-consciously) to the language of leadership (Learmonth and Griffin, in press). Perhaps the language of leadership can be understood, in part, as a defence against the anxieties that such negative portrayals might elicit.
2. What is the impact of gender on ideas about leadership? In spite of our relatively brief criticisms of women-in-leadership courses in Chapter 9, we have a feeling that the language of leadership appeals most strongly to those attracted to certain versions of (heroic) masculinity. In any case, the question of how gender might be implicated in the language of leadership in the specific sense in which we have used it in this book looks like a good empirical question for further investigation.
3. We have also been struck by the evident English-speaking bias in our book (as well as, incidentally by the Englishness of it more generally). There is, however, relatively little known about the effects of the language of leadership when the word in question is not 'leadership' but an equivalent term in another tongue. Do words generally translated into English as 'leadership' have the same sort of effects as we have outlined

here? Or is what we have been discussing in this book a phenomenon specific to the English language?
4. Finally, we have pretty self-consciously limited our analysis of the effects of the language of leadership to standard work settings. Although people like Daniel the shoe monitor we met in Chapter 2 have occasionally made an appearance, we wonder what its effects are in a non-work context – such as the family?

REFERENCES

Abrahamson, E., Berkowitz, H. and Dumez, H. (2016) A more relevant approach to relevance in management studies: an essay on performativity. *Academy of Management Review*, 41: 367–381.
Academy of Management (2018) Disney animated films may negatively influence children's perception of work. Available at: https://aom.org/News/Press-Releases/Disney-animated-films-may-negatively-influence-children-s-perception-of-work.aspx (Accessed 10th November 2018).
Adorno, T. (1951) *Freudian Theory and the Pattern of Fascist Propaganda*. Available at: https://cominsitu.files.wordpress.com/2018/01/theodor-w-adorno-freudian-theory-and-the-pattern-of-fascist-propaganda-5.pdf (Accessed 3rd October 2018).
Alvesson, M. (1996) Leadership studies: from procedure and abstraction to reflexivity and situation. *Leadership Quarterly*, 7: 455–485.
Alvesson, M., Blom, M. and Sveningsson, S. (2017) *Reflexive Leadership: Organising in an Imperfect World*. London: Sage.
Alvesson, M., Bridgman, T. and Willmott, H. (2011) *The Oxford Handbook of Critical Management Studies*. Oxford: Oxford University Press.
Alvesson, M. and Kärreman, D. (2016) Intellectual failure and ideological success in organization studies: the case of transformational leadership. *Journal of Management Inquiry*, 25: 139–152.
Alvesson, M. and Spicer, A. (2011) Theories of leadership. In: M. Alvesson and A. Spicer (eds.), *Metaphors We Lead By: Understanding Leadership in the Real World*. Abingdon: Routledge.
Alvesson, M. and Spicer, A. (2014) Critical perspectives on leadership. In: D.V. Day (ed.), *The Oxford Handbook of Leadership and Organizations*. Oxford: Oxford University Press.
Anderson, P. (2017) *The H-Word: The Peripeteia of Hegemony*. London: Verso.
Ashcraft, K.L. and Muhr, S.L. (2018) Coding military command as promiscuous practice: unsettling the gender binaries of leadership metaphors. *Human Relations*, 71: 206–228.
Austin, J.L. (1962) *How to Do Things with Words*. Oxford: Oxford University Press.

References

Barthes, R. (1967) *The Death of the Author*. Available at: www.tbook.constantvzw.org/wp-content/death_authorbarthes.pdf (Accessed 8th October 2018).

Bass, B.M. (1985) *Leadership and Performance Beyond Expectation*. New York: Free Press.

Beard, M. (2017) *Women & Power: A Manifesto*. London: Profile Books.

Bennis, W. (1989) *On Becoming a Leader*. London: Hutchinson Business Books.

Berghout, M.A., Oldenhof, L., Fabbricotti, I.N. and Hilders, C.G.J.M. (2018) Discursively framing physicians as leaders: institutional work to reconfigure medical professionalism. *Social Science & Medicine*, 212: 68–75.

Berlin, J.A. (1996) *Rhetorics, Poetics, and Cultures: Refiguring College English Studies*. Urbana, Ill.: National Council of Teachers of English.

Blom, M., and Alvesson, M. (2015) Less followership, less leadership? An inquiry into the basic but seemingly forgotten downsides of leadership. *M@n@gement*, 18: 266–282.

Bloom, P. and Rhodes, C. (2018) *CEO Society: The Corporate Takeover of Everyday Life*. London: Zed Books.

BNC (2017) *British National Corpus*. Available at: www.natcorp.ox.ac.uk/ (Accessed 1st August 2017).

Boltanski, L. and Chiapello, E. (2005) *The New Spirit of Capitalism* (Trans. G. Elliott) London: Verso.

Braverman, H. (1974) *Labor and Monopoly Capital: The Degradation of Work in the Twentieth Century*. New York: Monthly Review Press.

Bridgman, T., McLaughlin, C. and Cummings, S. (2018) Overcoming the problem of solving business problems: using theory differently to rejuvenate the case method for turbulent times. *Journal of Management Education*, 42: 441–460.

Brocklehurst, M., Grey, C. and Sturdy, A. (2010) Management: the work that dare not speak its name. *Management Learning*, 41: 7–19.

Burns, J.M. (1978/2010) *Leadership*. New York: Harper Collins. (Harper Perennial Political Classics Edition).

Butler, J. (1997) *Excitable Speech: A Politics of the Performative*. New York: Routledge.

Butler, N., Delaney, H. and Spoelstra, S. (2018) Risky business: reflections on critical performativity in practice. *Organization*, 25: 428–445.

Calás, M.B. and Smircich, L. (1991) Voicing seduction to silence leadership. *Organization Studies*, 12: 567–602.

Carroll, B., Firth, J. and Wilson, S. (eds) (2019) *After Leadership*. New York: Routledge.

Carroll, B., Ford, J. and Taylor, S. (eds) (2015) *Leadership: Contemporary Critical Perspectives*. London: Sage.

Clark, T., Wright, M., Iskoujina, Z. and Garnett, P. (2014) JMS at 50: trends over time. *Journal of Management Studies*, 51: 19–37.

Collinson, D. (1988) Engineering humour: masculinity, joking and conflict in shop floor relations. *Organization Studies*, 9: 181–199.

Collinson, D. (2011) Critical leadership studies. In: A. Bryman, D. Collinson, K. Grint and B. Jackson (eds), *The SAGE Handbook of Leadership*. London: Sage.

Collinson, D. (2014) Dichotomies, dialectics and dilemmas: new directions for critical leadership studies. *Leadership*, 10: 36–55.

Collinson, D. (2017) Critical leadership studies: a response to Learmonth and Morrell. *Leadership*, 13: 272–284.

Collinson, D., Jones, O.S. and Grint, K. (2018) 'No more heroes': critical perspectives on leadership romanticism. *Organization Studies*, 39: 1625–1647.

Collinson, D. and Tourish, D. (2015) Teaching leadership critically: new directions for leadership pedagogy. *Academy of Management Learning and Education*, 14: 576–594.

Conant Leadership (2017) Available at: https://conantleadership.com/4-leadership-quotes-that-hold-us-to-a-higher-standard/ (Accessed 4th October 2017).

Czarniawska, B. (2012) New plots are badly needed in finance: accounting for the financial crisis of 2007–2010. *Accounting, Auditing & Accountability Journal*, 25:756–775.

Davies, W. (2017) *The Limits of Neoliberalism: Authority, Sovereignty and the Logic of Competition*. (Revised Edition). London: Sage.

De Neve, J-E., Mikhaylov, S., Dawes, C.T., Christakis, N. A. and Fowler, J.H. (2013) Born to lead? A twin design and genetic association study of leadership role occupancy. *Leadership Quarterly*, 24: 45–60.

du Gay, P. (2000) *In Praise of Bureaucracy*. London: Sage.

Edgar, D. (2018) Jailbreak from the old order. *London Review of Books*, 40(8): 29–30.

ephemera (2014) *Special Issue: Management, Business, Anarchism*. Available at: www.ephemerajournal.org/sites/default/files/pdfs/issue/14-4ephemera-nov14.pdf#page=88 (Accessed 8th October 2018).

Fairclough, N. (1995) *Critical Discourse Analysis: The Critical Study of Language*. London: Longman.

Fehr, R., Yam, K.C. and Dang, C. (2015) Moralized leadership: the construction and consequences of ethical leader perceptions. *Academy of Management Review*, 40:182–209.

Fleming, P. and Spicer, A. (2003) Working at a cynical distance: implications for power, subjectivity and resistance. *Organization*, 10: 157–179.

Ford, J. and Harding, N. (2007) Move over management: we are all leaders now. *Management Learning*, 38: 475–493.

Ford, J. and Harding, N. (2018) Followers in leadership theory: fiction, fantasy and illusion. *Leadership*, 14: 3–24.

Ford, J., Harding, N. and Learmonth, M. (2008) *Leadership as Identity: Constructions and Deconstructions*. Houndmills: Palgrave Macmillan.

Foucault, M. (1991a) *Discipline and Punish: The Birth of the Prison*. London: Penguin.

Foucault, M. (1991b) Questions of method. In: G. Burchell, C. Gordan and J. Miller (eds) *The Foucault Effect: Studies in Governmentality with Two Lectures by and an Interview With Michel Foucault*. Chicago: The University of Chicago Press.

Foucault, M. (1996) The masked philosopher. In: S. Lotringer (ed) *Foucault Live: Collected Interviews, 1961–1984*. New York: Semiotext(e).

Foucault, M. (2000) Sexual choice, sexual act. In: P. Rabinow (ed) *Michel Foucault, Ethics, Subjectivity and Truth, Essential Works of Foucault 1945–1984 Volume One*. Harmondsworth, UK: Penguin.

Foucault, M. (2002) Interview with Michel Foucault. In: J. Faubion (ed) *Michel Foucault: Power, Essential Works of Foucault 1954–1984*. London: Penguin.

Foucault, M. (2006) *History of Madness*. (Trans: J. Khalfa and J. Murphy). New York: Routledge.

Fowler, R. (1991) *Language in the News: Discourse and Ideology in the Press*. New York: Routledge.

Freire, P. (1970/2017) *Pedagogy of the Oppressed*. London: Penguin.

Freud, S. (1922) *Group Psychology and the Analysis of the Ego*. Available at: http://freudians.org/wp-content/uploads/2014/09/Freud_Group_Psychology.pdf (Accessed 3rd October 2018).

Gemmill, G. and Oakley, J. (1992) Leadership: an alienating social myth? *Human Relations*, 45: 113–129.

Ghoshal, S. (2005) Bad management theories are destroying good management practices. *Academy of Management Learning & Education*, 4: 75–91.

Giridharadas, A. (2018) *Winners Take All: The Elite Charade of Changing the World*. London: Blackwell.

Glynn, M. and Raffaelli, R. (2010) Uncovering mechanisms of theory development in an academic field: lessons from leadership research. *Academy of Management Annals*, 4: 359–401.

Gond, J-P., Cabantous, L., Harding, N. and Learmonth, M. (2016) What do we mean by performativity in organizational and management theory? The uses and abuses of performativity. *International Journal of Management Reviews*, 18: 440–463.

Green, S. (2014) *Talent Management for Future Leaders and Leadership Development for Bishops and Deans: A New Approach*. Available at: www.churchofengland.org/media/2130591/report.pdf (Accessed 26th October 2017).

Griffin, M., Humphreys, M. and Learmonth, M. (2015a) Doing Free Jazz and free organizations, 'a certain experience of the impossible'? Ornette Coleman encounters Jacques Derrida. *Journal of Management Inquiry*, 24: 25–35.

Griffin, M., Learmonth, M. and Elliott, C. (2015b) Non-domination, contestation and freedom: the contribution of Philip Pettit to learning and democracy in organizations. *Management Learning*, 46: 317–336.

Grint, K. (2000) *The Arts of Leadership*. Oxford: Oxford University Press.

Grint, K. (2010) *Leadership: A Very Short Introduction*. Oxford: Oxford University Press.

Grint, K. (2011) The sacred in leadership: separation, sacrifice and silence. *Organization Studies*, 31: 89–107.

Grint, K., Jones, O.S. and Holt, C. (2017) What is leadership: person, result, position, purpose or process, or all or none of these? In: J. Storey, J. Hartley, J-L. Denis, P. t'Hart and D. Ulrich (eds), *The Routledge Companion to Leadership*. New York: Routledge.

Harding, N. (2014) Reading leadership through Hegel's master/slave dialectic: towards a theory of the powerlessness of the powerful. *Leadership*, 14: 391–411.

Harding, N., Lee, H., Ford, J. and Learmonth, M. (2011) Leadership and charisma: a desire that cannot speak its name? *Human Relations*, 64: 927–949.

Hargreaves, D. (2019) *Are Chief Executives Overpaid?* Cambridge: Polity Press.

Hendry, J. (2013) *Management: A Very Short Introduction*. Oxford: Oxford University Press.

Herman, A. (2009) *Gandhi and Churchill: The Epic Rivalry that Destroyed an Empire and Forged our Age*. London: Penguin.

Humphreys, M., Ucbasaran, D. and Lockett, A. (2012) Sensemaking and sensegiving stories of jazz leadership. *Human Relations*, 65: 41–62.

Jones, O. (2015) *The Establishment: And How They Get Away With It*. London: Penguin.

Kelly, S. (2008) Leadership: a categorical mistake? *Human Relations*, 61: 763–782.

Kelly, S. (2014) Towards a negative ontology of leadership. *Human Relations*, 67: 905–922.

Keynes, J.M. (1936) *The General Theory of Employment, Interest and Money*. London: MacMillan.

King, D. and Learmonth, M. (2015) Can critical management studies ever be 'practical'? A case study in engaged scholarship. *Human Relations*, 68: 353–375.

Klein, M. (2016) *Democratizing Leadership: Counter-Hegemonic Democracy in Organizations, Institutions and Communities*. Charlotte, NC: Information Age Publishing.

Krantz, J. and Gilmore, T.N. (1990) The splitting of leadership and management as a social defense. *Human Relations*, 43: 183–204.

Learmonth, M. (2005) Doing things with words: the case of 'management' and 'administration'. *Public Administration*, 83: 617–637.

Learmonth, M. and Humphreys, M. (2011) Blind spots in Dutton, Roberts and Bednar's 'pathways for positive identity construction at work': 'you've got to accentuate the positive, eliminate the negative'. *Academy of Management Review*, 36: 424–427.

Learmonth, M. and Griffin, M. (in press) Fiction and the identity of the manager. In: A.D. Brown (ed) *The Oxford Handbook of Identities in Organizations*. Oxford: Oxford University Press.

Learmonth, M. and Morrell, K. (2017) Is critical leadership studies 'critical'? *Leadership*, 13: 257–271.

Lemoine, G.J., Hartnall, C.A. and Leroy, H. (2018) Taking stock of moral approaches to leadership: an integrative review of ethical, authentic and servant leadership. *Academy of Management Annals*, 13, doi:10.5465/annals.2016.0121.

Liu, H. and Baker, C. (2016) White knights: leadership as the heroicisation of whiteness. *Leadership*, 12: 420–488.

Mabey, C. and Knights, D. (eds) (2018) *Leadership Matters: Finding Voice, Connection and Meaning in the 21st Century*. New York: Routledge.

McCann, G. (2015) From management to leadership. In: S. Edgell, H. Gottfried and E. Granter (eds), *The SAGE Handbook of the Sociology of Work and Employment*. London: Sage.

McDonald, D. (2017) *The Golden Passport: Harvard Business School, the Limits of Capitalism, and the Moral Failure of the MBA Elite*. New York: Harper Collins.

March, J.G. (2005) Mundane organizations and heroic leaders. In J.G. March and T. Weil (eds), *On Leadership*. Malden, MA: Blackwell.

March, J. (2018) Heroes and history: lessons for leadership from Tolstoy's War and Peace. Available at: www.gsb.stanford.edu/insights/heroes-history-lessons-leadership-tolstoys-war-peace (Accessed 3rd October 2018).

Martin, G. and Learmonth, M. (2012) A critical account of the rise and spread of 'leadership': the case of UK health care. *Social Science & Medicine*, 74: 281–288.

Marx, K. and Engels, F. (1848/2012) *The Communist Manifesto*. London: Verso. Also available at: www.marxists.org/archive/marx/works/download/pdf/Manifesto.pdf (Accessed 5th November 2018).

Mautner, G. (2005) The entrepreneurial university: a discursive profile of a higher education buzzword. *Critical Discourse Studies*, 2: 95–120.

Mautner, G. (2007) Mining large corpora for social information: the case of 'elderly'. *Language in Society*, 36: 51–72.

Mautner, G. (2010) *Language and the Market Society: Critical Reflections on Discourse and Dominance*. New York: Routledge.

Mautner, G. (2015) *Discourse and Management: Critical Perspectives though the Language Lens*. Basingstoke: Palgrave MacMillan.

Meindl, J.R., Ehrlich, S.B. and Dukerich, J.M. (1985) The romance of leadership. *Administrative Science Quarterly*, 30: 78–102.

Moisander, J., Groß, C. and Eräranta, K. (2017) Mechanisms of biopower and neo-liberal governmentality in precarious work: mobilizing the dependent self-employed as independent business owners. *Human Relations*, 7, doi:10.1177/0018726717718918.

Morley, L. (2013) The rules of the game: women and the leaderist turn in higher education. *Gender & Education*, 25: 116–131.

Morrell, K. (2004) Socratic dialogue as a tool for teaching business ethics. *Journal of Business Ethics*, 53: 383–392.

Morrell, K. (2012) *Organization, Society and Politics: An Aristotelian Perspective*. New York: Palgrave Macmillan.

Morrell, K. and Hartley, J. (2006) A model of political leadership. *Human Relations*, 59: 483–504.

Morrell, K. and Learmonth, M. (2015) Against evidence-based management, for management learning. *Academy of Management Learning & Education*, 14: 520–533.

Morrell, K., Learmonth, M. and Heracleous, L. (2015) An archaeological critique of 'evidence-based management': one digression after another. *British Journal of Management*, 26: 529–543.

Morrison, B. (2003) Officer class. *The Guardian*. Available at: www.theguardian.com/world/2003/apr/03/iraq.military1 (Accessed 25th April 2018).

Mould, O. (2018) *Against Creativity: Everything You Have Been Told About Creativity is Wrong*. London: Verso.

Nichols, J. (2014) Tony Benn and the five essential questions of democracy. *The Nation*. Available at: www.thenation.com/article/tony-benn-and-five-essential-questions-democracy/ (Accessed 29th October 2018).

Noor, P. (2017) Zero help for those who need it. *The Guardian*. Available at: www.pressreader.com/uk/the-guardian/20170715/282291025280101 (Accessed 27th May 2017).

O'Reilly, D. and Reed, M.I. (2010) 'Leaderism': an evolution of managerialism in UK public service reform. *Public Administration*, 88: 960–978.

Orwell, G. (1938/2000) *Homage to Catalonia*. London: Penguin Classics.

Orwell, G. (1945/2000) *Animal Farm: A Fairy Story*. London: Penguin Classics.

Orwell, G. (1945/2013) *Politics and the English Language*. London: Penguin Classics.

Ospina, S.M., Foldy, E.G., Fairhurst, G.T. and Jackson, B. (2018) Special issue call for papers: collective dimensions of leadership: the challenges of connecting theory and method. *Human Relations*. Available at: www.tavinstitute.org/humanrelations/special_issues/LeadershipCollectiveDimensions.html (Accessed 2nd July 2018).

O'Ween, H. (2013) *Decoding Leadership Bullshit*. Vienna: Page Publishing.

Parker, M. (2002) *Against Management: Organization in the Age of Managerialism*. Cambridge: Polity Press.

Parker, M. (2018) *Shut Down the Business School: An Insider's Account of What's Wrong with Management Education*. London: Pluto Press.

Perren, L. and Dannreuther, C. (2012) Political signification of the entrepreneur: temporal analysis of constructs, agency and reification. *International Small Business Journal*, 31: 603–628.

Petriglieri, G. and Petriglieri, J.L. (2015) Can business schools humanize leadership? *Academy of Management Learning & Education*, 14: 625–647.

Pfeffer, J. (2015a) Why the leadership industry has failed. Available at: www.gsb.stanford.edu/insights/jeffrey-pfeffer-why-leadership-industry-has-failed (Accessed 23rd July 2018).

Pfeffer, J. (2015b) *Leadership BS: Fixing Workplaces and Careers One Truth at a Time*. New York: Harper Collins.

Plutarch (no date) *The Life of Alexander*. Available at: http://penelope.uchicago.edu/Thayer/E/Roman/Texts/Plutarch/Lives/Alexander*/3.html (Accessed 18th February 2019).

Pollach, I. (2012) Taming textual data: the contribution of corpus linguistics to computer-aided text analysis. *Organizational Research Methods*, 15: 263–287.

Raelin, J.A. (ed) (2016a) *Leadership-As-Practice: Theory and Application*. New York: Routledge.

Raelin, J.A. (2016b) Introduction. In: J.A. Raelin (ed), *Leadership-As-Practice: Theory and Application*. New York: Routledge.

Return to Now (2017) https://returntonow.net/2017/09/22/85-people-hate-jobs-gallup-poll-says/ (Accessed 5th October 2018).

Rivkin, J. and Ryan, M. (1998) *Literary Theory: An Anthology*. London: Blackwell.

Rost, J.C. (1991) *Leadership for the Twenty-First Century*. Westport, CT: Praeger Publishers.

Sainsbury's (2018) www.sainsburys.jobs/leaders (Accessed 27th August 2018).

Sandhurst (2017) *Serve to Lead*. Available at: www.mkbartlett.co.uk/data/further/0311MOIFR01.pdf (Accessed 2nd October 2017).

Scothorne, R. (2018) Pop your own abscess. *London Review of Books*, 40(4): 40–41.

Selznick, P. (1957) *Leadership in Administration: A Sociological Perspective*. Berkley, Ca: University of California Press.

Sheffield, G.D. (2000) *Leadership in the Trenches: Officer-Man Relations, Morale and Discipline in the British Army in the Era of the First World War*. Houndmills: MacMillan Press.

Sinclair, A. (2014) A feminist case for leadership. In: J. Damousi, K. Rubenstein and M. Tomsic (eds) *Diversity in Leadership: Australian Women Past and Present*. Sidney: Australian National University Press.

Sinek, S. (2014) *Leaders Eat Last: Why Some Teams Pull Together and Others Don't*. New York: Penguin.

Sketchengine (2017) www.sketchengine.co.uk/ (Accessed 1st August 2017).

Smircich, L. and Morgan, G. (1982) Leadership: the management of meaning. *The Journal of Applied Behavioral Science*, 18: 257–273.

Smyth, J. (2017) *The Toxic University: Zombie Leadership, Academic Rock Stars and Neo-liberal Ideology*. London: Palgrave.

Spicer, A. (2018) *Business Bullshit*. New York: Routledge.

Spoelstra, S. (2018) *Leadership and Organization: A Philosophical Introduction*. New York: Routledge.

Steger, M.B. and Roy, R.K. (2010) *Neo-liberalism: A Very Short Introduction*. Oxford: Oxford University Press.

Storey, J., Hartley, J., Denis, J-L., t'Hart, P. and Ulrich, D. (2017a) Preface. In: J. Storey, J. Hartley, J-L. Denis, P. t'Hart and D. Ulrich (eds), *The Routledge Companion to Leadership*. New York: Routledge.

Storey, J., Hartley, J., Denis, J-L., t'Hart, P. and Ulrich, D. (2017b) *The Routledge Companion to Leadership*. New York: Routledge.

TGI Fridays (2018) About TGI Fridays UK Limited. Available at: www.b.co.uk/company-profile/?t.g.i.-friday%27s-uk-ltd-47412 (Accessed 23rd May 2018).

The Woman Who Fell to Earth (2018) www.planetclaire.tv/quotes/doctorwho/series-eleven/the-woman-who-fell-to-earth/ (Accessed 18th October 2018).

Tourish, D. (2013) *The Dark Side of Transformational Leadership: A Critical Perspective*. New York: Routledge.

Tourish, D. (2015) Some announcements, reaffirming the critical ethos of Leadership, and what we look for in submissions. *Leadership*, 11: 135–141.

Tutchell, E. and Edmonds, J. (2015) *Man-Made: Why So Few Women are in Positions of Power*. Surrey: Gower.

Tutchell, E. and Edmonds, J. (2018) *The Stalled Revolution: Is Equality for Women an Impossible Dream?* Bingley: Emerald.

Uhl-Bien, M., Riggio, R.E., Lowe, K.B. and Carsten, M.K. (2014) Followership theory: a review and research agenda. *Leadership Quarterly*, 25: 83–104.

Weber, M. (1948) The sociology of charismatic authority. In H.H. Gerth and C. Wright Mills (eds), *From Max Weber: Essays in Sociology*. London: Routledge.

White, H. (1973) *Metahistory: The Historical Imagination in the Nineteenth Century*. Baltimore: Johns Hopkins University Press.

Whyte, W. H. (1957) *The Organization Man*. London: Pelican.

Wilson, S. (2016) *Thinking Differently about Leadership: A Critical History of Leadership Studies*. Cheltenham: Edward Elgar.

World Economic Forum (2018) Available at: www.weforum.org/about/world-economic-forum (Accessed 30th April 2018).
Wright Mills, C.M. (1956) *The Power Elite*. Oxford: Oxford University Press.
Zaretsky, E. (2018) The mass psychology of Trumpism. *LRB Blog*. Available at: www.lrb.co.uk/blog/2018/09/18/eli-zaretsky/the-mass-psychology-of-trumpism/ (Accessed 1st October 2018).
Zoller, H.M. and Fairhurst, G.T. (2007) Resistance leadership: the overlooked potential in critical and leadership studies. *Human Relations*, 60: 1331–1360.

INDEX

Note: entries in *italics* denote figures; entries in **bold** denote tables.

academic journals 102–3, 119, 123, 144–7
academic leadership 16–19; *see also* HE; universities
Academy of Management Review 103
administration: as leadership 16, 18, 20; reclaiming term 131–3
Adorno, Theodor 142
Alexander the Great 72, 87
Alvesson, Mats 21, 126
AOM (Academy of Management) 119–20, 137, *138*
Aristotle 65, 72
Austin, John 8, 77–8
authentic leaders 3, 40
the author, death of 63–4

Bader, Douglas 88
Barthes, Roland 147
Beard, Mary 130
Bennis, Warren 95–6
Berlin, James 58
Blair, Tony 53, 94–5
BNC (British National Corpus) 7, 28
Boltanski, Luc 98, 102
bosses: descriptive terms for 42; flattering 1, 4–5, 33, 39–41, 51, 102, 111–12, 133; increased power of 53; and leadership 21, 37–9; worker attitudes to 2 (*see also* employment relationship)
Braverman, Harry 143

British Army 84, 87, 89, 91
British English, corpora of 7, 28–9
Broms, Robin 91
Burke, James 103
Burns, James MacGregor 39, 94
business leaders 17, 30, 42, 144
business schools: job advertisements for 16; language of leadership in 44, 120, 144; opposition to 141; promoting CEOs 109; women-in-leadership programmes 129
Butler, Judith 123–4, 147
Butler, Nick 138

capitalism: defenders of 53; and leadership 1, 124; resistance to 98, 102
celebritization 105
CEOs (Chief Executive Officers): academics advising 138; descriptive terms for 42; as leaders 26, 39, 47, 52, 95, 102–4; and military leaders 91–2; pay of 35, 41, 114; relationship with staff 35–6, 112–13, 115; women as 128
charismatic authority 142
Chiapello, Eve 98, 102
chivalry 97
Churchill, Winston 93, 103–4
class, social 91
Clinton, Bill 94–5
closed systems 61

CLS (critical leadership studies) 9, 121–3, 138; further reading on 140; and leadership-as-practice 127; writing in 33, 125
CMS (Critical Management Studies) 120, 122, 124
collective leadership 9, 127
Collinson, David 33–5, **34**, 37, 109, 122–3, 125–6, 143
collocational profiles 29
commercialization, resisting 40
Communist Manifesto, The 114
compassionate leaders 40, 133
consent, freely-given 89–90
consultancy 25, 52, 138
corporate language 71–4, 76
corporate leadership 128, 140
corporate power xiv, 5, 49–51, 72–3, 104, 135, 139
corpus linguistics (CL) 28, 33, 38, 115, 143
counter-cultural movements 97–8
critical leadership studies *see* CLS
cultural identities 35
cynicism: about language of leadership 2, 44; about leadership xii–xiv; positive 71–2, 130–3

De Neve, Jan-Emmanuel 102
Delaney, Helen 138
democracy 38, 92–4, 127
Derrida, Jacques 147
Diogenes 71–2, 87
discourse: constitutive effects of 73; use of term 67
discursive practices 75–7
doctors, and leadership 40

economics language 74–6
elite values, traditional 98
elites: business and organizational xiii–xiv, 2, 6, 8–9, 100–2, 121; leaders as 24–5, 34, 37, 47, 109, 123; and neo-liberalism xiv; projected identities of 51, 92, 105; and revolutionaries 84–5
Ellington, Duke 38, 143
emancipatory leadership 98, 102, 137, 148
emplotment 64
employment relationship 7, 45–50, 53, 143
English language 149–50; *see also* British English
English Web 2015 7, 28
enmeshed dilemma 67

entrepreneurship 60, 135–6; further reading on 149
episodic power 50
The Establishment 42
everyday power 50–1, 53, 132
expectations, living up to 38, 66; *see also* Pygmalion effect

Facebook 105
Fairhurst, Gail 122
fascism *see* right-wing authoritarianism
Fehr, Ryan 104
feminism 57, 83, 130
followers 2; academic use of term 109–10, 123–6; cultural resonance of term xii, 19; leaders as having 4, 21–2, 45–6, 79, 88, 111–12 (*see also* leader/follower dyad); negative connotations of 90, 110–11, 113; organizational use of term 38–9, 111–13; relationship with leaders xiii, 5–6, 23, 48, 108; on social media 106–7, 110; word sketch of use **111**
followership, critique of 148
football punditry 15, 21, 24, 44
Forrester, Karen 35, 37
Foucault, Michel 8, 76, 133–4, 141
Fowler, Roger 58
Freire, Paulo 84–5, 101–2
Freud, Sigmund 2, 142
From Here to Eternity 90

Gandhi, Mahatma 99, 103–4
Gates, Bill 103
gender, and leadership 90–1, 149; *see also* women's leadership
Ghoshal, Sumantra 75
glamorization: of bosses 34, 39, 133; of elites xiii, 4, 6, 121, 129; of military leaders 92; of the mundane 136
Glynn, Mary Ann 99
Golem effect 75, 78
Graham, Laurie 122
Greece, Ancient 72, 87–8
Gregory, Andrew 91
Grint, Keith: on associations of leadership 44; criticism of 143; defining leadership 21–4, 26, 37, 88, 112; and heroism 92; and management 33; on military leadership 89
group leader 30
gurus xii, 21, 95, 106

Index

Harding, Nancy 123–5
Hargreaves, Deborah 41
HBS (Harvard Business School) 144
HE (higher education): language of leadership in 16–20, **17–18**, 24, 132; *see also* universities
Hegel, G. W. F. 123–4
hegemony 143
Hendry, John 5
hippie leadership 8, 87, 95–8, 148
history, textuality of 63–4, 67
Hitler, Adolf 93, 99, 142
humanities 8, 61–4, 147
humble-bragging 106–7, 132

identities, as discursive 78–9
Instagram 110
Iraq War 91, 94, 132

jargon 63, 120
jazz bands 38
job descriptions, language of leadership in 7, 16, **17–18**, 20
job interviews xii, 131–2
Jobs, Steve 103

Kant, Immanuel 19
Kärreman, Dan 126, 141
Keynes, John Maynard 75
King, Martin Luther, Jr. 98, 103–4
knowledge, Foucault on 76
knowledge leadership 23

labels, impact of xiii–xiv, 57–8, 60, 65–6, 74
language: function of 57–8, 62–5, 148; performative and constative 77; revolutionary 101–2; role in organizations 73–4; social science on 61, 67 (*see also* linguistic turn); *see also* ordinary language
language communities 73
language of leadership x–xiii, **3**; academic use of 123–6, 138–9, 144–7; beliefs behind 1–2, 100–1; challenging xiii–xiv, 45, 69, 131–4; changes in use of 25–32; and corporate power 49–54, 103–4, 121; and employment relationship 33–5, 44, 46–9, 143; further reading on 142; further research questions on 149–50; future prospects for 139; and philosophy of language 63, 78–9; popularity of 6, 13–16, 20; and realities of work 4–6, 35–7, 40–2, 72, 102; as self-fulfilling prophecy 66–7; ubiquity of 119–20, 131, 136–7; use of term 2–3; *see also* leader-shit
leader, word sketch of term 29, **30**
leader-centrism 3, 110
leader/follower dyad 33, 124–7
leaders, people who some have called **99**
Leadership (journal) 21, 123–5
leadership: against xii, 48, 54; as being in front 85–6; blanket positivity of 83–5, 99–100, 104, 110; celebration of 52, 121, 136; as default term 58–9; as discourse 76–7; further reading on 140–1; as inspirational 95–8; performing 70–1, 75; pro-elite connotations of 24–5, 34, 37–42, 45–6, 52, 104–5, 135; reinventing 120–1; relabelling activities as 139; romance of 121; as science 59–60; strong 13, **14**, 21; trouble defining 21–4, 27; use of term 2–6, 14–15
leadership academics 21, 59, 113, 138; *see also* CLS
leadership chatter 105–6
leadership development x, 15, 26, 52, 119, 127
leadership failures 13, **14**, 21
leadership industry xii, 4, 25–6, 105
Leadership Quarterly 102, 108, 124–5, 147
leadership research x, 22, 25, 108–10, 125; *see also* CLS
leadership style xii, 25, 129, 138
Leadership Summit 24–5
leadership teams 15, 119–20
leadership-as-practice 127–8
leader-shit 44, 131–3, 137–8
Lewinsky, Monica 94
linguistic turn 62–5, 67, 73–4; and its descendants **68–9**
LinkedIn 9, 96, 105–6, 133
lived experience 20, 78, 98
Lockwood, Al 91

Mackey, John 103–4
management: academic institutions using term **145–6**; associations of term 4–5, 37–40, 83, 104; critical perspective on 50 (*see also* CMS); definition of 60; language of 5, 28, 44, 51, 53, 105, 144; of meaning 121; relationship with workers 108; as science 59–61; study and practice of 74–5; value of term 45–6

management and leadership: inversion of 108–9; in the military 84–5, 91–2; political 94; revolutionary 101–2; significance of shift between 51–3; subordinates and followers 112; as synonymous 6, 21–3, 25–7, 33–4, 43–4, 114, 123–4, 141–2
management studies 59, 61–2, 74–5; *see also* CLS
managers: use of term xi, 132; word sketch of use **31**, 32
Mandela, Nelson 98
Martin, Graham 139
Marx, Karl 114, 143
masculinity, heroic 90–1, 94, 139, 149
Maslow's hierarchy of needs 23
May 1968 student uprising 98, 102
meaning as use 63, 70
me-dership 9, 105–8, **107**
mega-discourse 126
Meindl, James R. 121
metalanguage 67
micro-resistance 132, 139
military leadership 2, 8, 83–4, 88–93; further reading on 148; and inspiration 96–7; and other ranks 113; and political leadership 86–7, 93–4
minority groups 79, 128
Montrose, Louis 64
Morrison, Blake 91–2, 132
Mother Theresa 103

narcissism 107
natural language philosophers *see* ordinary language, philosophy of
natural science 59, 62
Nazi Germany 85
neo-liberalism: lack of pluralism in 131; and language of leadership xiv–1, 25, 51–3, 135, 143, 149; and me-dership 108
new rhetoric 65, 68
non-coercive relationships 37, 39

officer class 91
open systems 61
ordinary language: databases of 28, 33; philosophy of 62–3, 65, 70, 77
O'Reilly, Dermot 32
Organization Man 97
organization studies 32, 60, 143, 147–8
organizational leadership: critics of 98, 121; further reading on 141–2; future of 139; and military leadership 85, 88; and neo-liberalism 53; and political leadership 95
organizational life, being at the front in 86
Orwell, George: *Animal Farm* x, xii–xiii, 46–8, 83; *Homage to Catalonia* 92–3; on language and power xiii–1, 3–4, 13, 44, 133, 135

performativity 75, 77–9, 147–8
Petriglieri, Gianpiero and Jennifer 5
physics 59–62
political leadership 8, 32, 38, 86–7, 93–5, 97–8, 140
positive organizational theory 136
poverty 41, 123
power: asymmetries 71, 121; and language 73; modes of 49–50
power elite 42; *see also* elites
profits xiii, 5, 47, 49, 73, 102, 107
project leaders 30
psychology, social 8, 65
Pygmalion effect 65–7, 70, 75, 78

Raelin, Joseph 127
Raffaelli, Ryan 99
readymade language: function of 2–4, 58; of leadership 6, 8, 21, 34, 40, 79, 113, 128; Orwell on xiii, 1, 13, 44, 135
Reed, Mike 32
reflexivity 125
resistance leadership 122–3, 128
revolutionary leadership 84, 101, 122
rhetoric 8, 64–5; of hard work 41; management and leadership 51
right-wing authoritarianism 114–15, 142
Rost, Joseph 26–7, 31, 33, 109, 111

Sandhurst 84, 91
Santa's workshop 7, 46, 48, 108, 133
Schumpeter, Joseph 136
science: academic preoccupation with 8, 147; hierarchy of **59**, 60–2, 76
Scott, Walter 97
self-delusion 67, 97
self-fulfilling prophecies 8, 65–6, 75, 78
self-management 128
Selznick, Philip 95
senior leadership 25, 30–1, 52, 129
senior staff 6, 24, 32, 40
servant leadership 22, 40–1, 101, 132–3
Sinclair, Amanda 130

Sinek, Simon 85, 89, 101
Sketchengine 29
social media: leadership chatter on 96, 105–7; and use of language 9, 32
social science 19, 59, 62, 67, 75
Socrates 134
Spanish Civil War 92–3
speech act theory 77–8
Spicer, Andre 21
Spoelstra, Sverre 138, 141
Stalin, Joseph 83, 93
strategy 3, 93–5, 107, 120

Taylor, F. W. 23
team leader, use of term xi, 29, 71
teams, use of term 70–1
TGI Fridays 35–7, 47, 112–13
Tourish, Dennis 109, 125–6
trade unions 38, 45, 52–3, 95, 104, 122–3
transactional leadership 26, 94, 141
transformational leadership 26, 68, 94, 101, 141
Trump, Donald 95, 142
Twitter 105, 110

Uhl-Bien, Mary 108–11
uncertainty 22–3, 60, 76
universities: and entrepreneurship 136; language of leadership in 16–20, 40, 131, 133, 143; *see also* HE

Vernon, Chris 91
virtue signalling 97

wages 35–6, 41, 46–7, 49, 114
Weber, Max 2, 142
WEF (World Economic Forum) 95
whiteness, and leadership 91
Whyte, William H. 97
Wilson, Sloan 97
Winnet, Mike 9
women's leadership 9, 84, 128–30, 148–9
work, definition of 60
work organizations: conflict of interests in 35–7, 46–9, 51; depoliticizing 33–5; discourse within 73; leadership in xii, 1–2, 24, 79; and the military 89–90; power relations in 4–6, 38–9, 49–50, 73–4, 131 (*see also* employment relationship)
workers: attitude to bosses 2 (*see also* employment relationship); cultural identities 35; euphemistic language for 49; flattening 4–5, 7, 33, 133; as followers 9, 23, 34–5, 38–9, 41–2, 108–15, 123; as leaders 101–2; pay and conditions for 6–7, 35–6, 40, 52, 114; word sketch of use **115**
world leaders *see* political leadership
World War I 89–90
World War II 85, 88, 97

Zoller, Heather 122

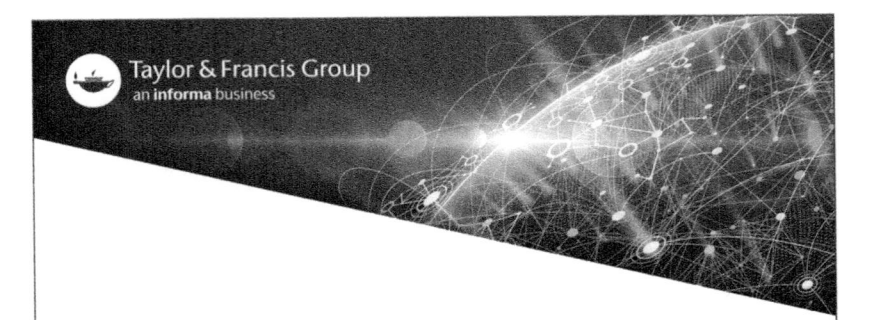